NEVER CHASE A PAYCHECK AGAIN

_____

Robert J. Watkins

NEVER CHASE A PAYCHECK AGAIN
Copyright © 2011 by Robert J. Watkins

This book may be purchased for educational, business or sales promotional purposes. For curriculum and seminar information please write to:

Conquer Worldwide Publishers
3600 Dallas Hwy, Ste 230
PMB 227
Marietta, GA 30064 USA
+1.888.378.5554 (tel)
+1.404.601.9692 (fax)
info@conquerworldwide.com (email)

FIRST EDITION

ISBN 978-0-615-3581-0

PRAISE FOR
Never Chase A Paycheck Again

"*Never Chase a Paycheck Again* is one of those books I wish I had read when I was 22 years old. It's filled with principles and practices that will help you achieve financial freedom. I highly recommend this important book for everyone."

> Os Hillman, President
> Marketplace Leaders
> Author of *TGIF Today God Is First*

"Wow, I simply love this book. Seldom does a book say it better or more powerfully than *Never Chase A Paycheck Again*. This book is a must read for those who want to navigate the slippery slope of financial freedom and self sufficiency. My heartfelt thanks go out to Robert Watkins for giving us this important and timely gem."

> George C. Fraser
> Author, *Success Runs In Our Race* and *Click*

"God's people will never reach their full potential for advancing His kingdom until the spirit of poverty. I am elated that Robert Watkins has now stepped forward and given us a practical toolbox for dismantling poverty in his dynamic book, *Never Chase a Paycheck Again*. I love this book, and so will you!"

C. Peter Wagner, Chancellor
Wagner Leadership Institute

"Robert Watkins' practical insights could not only make you a financial success, but help you launch your God-given purpose. *Never Chase A Paycheck Again* will help you do just that."

Dr. Samuel R. Chand, President Emeritus
Beulah Heights University

"Robert Watkins has written a comprehensive and inspiring step-by-step masterpiece. A must read for all of us who need money and relationships to secure our visions, families, ministries and businesses."

Lee Jenkins, author/consultant
Lee Jenkins Financial Group

"Tired of being stuck in a nowhere j.o.b.-Just Over Broke? Then this book is your key to future financial freedom. Read it then do it. Robert Watkins will be your financial coach."

-Dr. Larry Keefauver, President
VanKeef Financial, Inc.
Best-selling Author of over 30 books

TABLE OF CONTENTS

DEDICATION

This book is dedicated to every aspiring entrepreneur and future leader working tirelessly to take care of their families and improve their current circumstances. You inspired me to write this book.

ACKNOWLEDGEMENTS

Every book I write is an unselfish act of teamwork; and this one is no exception. I'd like to acknowledge the people who have been instrumental in my life.

- Evelyn Watkins, my beautiful wife of 18 years and my best friend. Thank you for constantly sharing your advice, wisdom and love with me. You've made me a better man.

- Gabrielle Watkins, my ambitious, loquacious and lovely 11 year-old daughter. Thank you, Gabrielle, for being an extraordinary young leader, a wise young lady and lots of fun.

- Noelle Watkins, my talented, gifted and clever 7-year-old daughter. Thank you, Noelle, for teaching me all over again how to love life and how to laugh at myself.

- Most important, God. Thank you, Lord, for keeping me alive to finish YOUR work.

CHAPTER SUMMARIES

1. AVOID GOING BROKE

Becoming a billionaire may or may not be your financial goal, but having more than enough money for your future should be. If you are willing to educate yourself financially and follow my simple six-step plan, your financial condition can begin steadily improving.

2. BUILD YOUR LIFE ON PURPOSE

The greatest disaster in a person's life is not death, but a life lived without purpose. The day you discover your *raison d'être* and begin to focus on your God-given gifts, skills, and talents; your life will change. You will stop chasing paychecks and experience money chasing you.

3. DEVELOP HEALTHY FINANCIAL HABITS

Unhealthy habits interfere with cash flow; the life blood of any successful financial game plan. To become financially stable, your habits must be intentional. I'll give you my six tried-and-true techniques to boost your cash flow without resorting to such drastic measures as selling your home, bailing out of your long-term investments or pawning your jewelry.

4. CREATE YOUR OWN INCOME

Creating your own income should be one of your primary goals in life. If you are earning at least $25,000 a year, you have the potential to earn over a million dollars in your lifetime. However, the sooner you shift your focus on creating income without your personal involvement, the sooner you can achieve personal and financial freedom.

5. SOLVE PROBLEMS AND GET PAID

Money is a reward for solving a problem in someone's life. Solving problems provides income, influence and financial provision. The precise problem you have been gifted to solve may not have anything to do with your current vocation or education. I'll show you how to make the transition.

6. FROM EMPLOYEE TO ENTREPRENEUR

You were created to lead, not follow. Entrepreneurial-minded people make things happen around them. This chapter is about possessing the right mindset for long-term success and learning the differences between being entrepreneur-minded and employee-minded. Being employee-minded can lead to a life of chasing a paycheck.

7. CONFIDENCE MAKES THE DIFFERENCE

Self-confidence is key to never chasing a paycheck again. People who lack self-confidence work for and follow people with high self-confidence. The **good news** is self-confidence can be learned, developed and maximized. In this chapter, you learn how to have the right amount of self-confidence to take informed risks, stretch yourself (but not beyond your abilities) and find success.

8. MAKE YOUR MONEY WORK FOR YOU

When applied prudently and shrewdly, money can become a very diligent employee. In this chapter, you will find many proven income-producing ideas to help you uncover opportunities and provide what I call "income insight". Income insight is where you see an opportunity to make money that other people cannot see.

9. CONQUERING THE LAST ENEMY

Courage means controlling your fear. Fear causes people to do what is comfortable, normal and easy. A life driven by love is expressed as desire, and strong desire will allow you to take calculated risks, help others and try new things.

Afterword

LIVE LIFE ON YOUR OWN TERMS

INTRODUCTION

Facing The Future with Confidence

I'm often struck with grief as I enter Wal-Mart Superstores. As I walked through the doors on one particular day, I noticed the deep aging lines on the face of the elderly door-greeter.

Now in his "golden years", he appeared to be forced by his financial circumstances to work for just above minimum wage. A fearful thought entered my mind as I envisioned myself as that elderly door greeter; working at low wages to make ends meet.

While a majority of these Wal-Mart greeters appear happy to have a job, I am certain they didn't dream of working as a minimum wage door-greeters in their "golden years." Did an unexpected event take place in their lives that wiped out their life savings or were they simply unprepared for the future? Either way, I doubt if chasing a paycheck beyond retirement age is ever a life-time financial goal.

Having adequate income at retirement is not the only problem facing many people today. People have trouble providing the daily basics for their families. Why are so many people facing financial trouble in the richest country in the world? What can you do to not only avoid going broke but become financially prosperous even in an uncertain economy? With so many people competing for so few jobs, how can you insure resources for your family now and for yourself in the future? This book will answer all of these questions and others.

Statistics show that we are indeed in an economic crisis. But that does not give us an excuse to remain poor and unproductive with our lives. Instead we need to seek out unconventional ways to make our money work for us. I want you to be in a position to enjoy life now and look forward to a financially secure future.

Before I offer some practical ways to avoid going broke in today's economy, I want to share a few statistics. You will realize the importance of establishing sound financial practices in your life starting today. The following statistics are alarming, but I share this information so that you can break free of what's holding you back rather than you becoming a negative statistic.

1. According to the U.S. Department of Labor, more than 2.6 million people lost their jobs in the United States in 2008. This created a need to seek non-traditional ways to make money to support their families and avoid bankruptcy.

2. In 2007 the U.S. Census Bureau reported that half of the American households were living on less than $48,200 a year. This makes a comfortable retirement difficult for most people with a family.

Thanks to advancements in medicine and technology, our average life span continues to increase while the average bank account fails to increase at a comparable rate.

Why are some people able to thrive even in this down economy while others find it difficult to even supply the basic needs of life? The answer lies in the following pages of this book. By studying what successful people do with their money, thinking uncommonly for ways to generate your own income and planning for your future you can become a positive rather than a negative statistic.

If you are ready to move forward and start living a rich life of personal freedom and purpose, grab a pen and a notepad and prepare to learn a new lifestyle. I will share with you how I went from employee to entrepreneur, from poverty to prosperity and from month-to-month living to wealthy.

Stop chasing a paycheck and start living your life as you were equipped and designed to live. As you do you will move from poverty to prosperity, from poor to rich in more than just your finances.

The end of each chapter has a summarized list of Financial Principles and exercises you can implement immediately. When you implement these principles, and continue to do them, your life will change forever.

You will be amazed at how simple this plan really is!

Life Changing Answers Available in This Chapter

- How do I avoid going broke when my income is dwindling?

- What is a sure-fire plan to ensure I don't go broke?

- How can I develop a workable financial game plan in this economy?

Chapter 1

AVOID GOING BROKE

Living life on your own terms begins with an effective game plan.

Here is an interesting fact that may surprise you. Most of us can live debt-free and become millionaires regardless of our circumstances. According to a Chicago based research firm, the Spectrem Group, the number of households worth $1 million grew 21% to 7.5 million in the last few years. How would you like to become a member of this fast growing affluent group? I believe you can.

It Starts With The Way You Think

Wealthy people "adopt" certain attitudes towards life which help them to avoid going broke. Aspiring to live the lifestyles of a Donald Trump, Bill Gates or George Soros may not be your goal, but you can avoid going broke and prosper financially. Let's examine the 5 attitudes of wealthy people that you need to avoid going broke.

1. **Adopt a "business" attitude**

The Federal Reserve says that of the top 10% of the most affluent individuals in the U.S. own all or part of at least one privately held business. Only 12% of the remaining 90% of American families own all or part of a business.

Adopting a "business attitude" means you look for ways to solve problems in your community and charge a reasonable fee for your service or product. Now, more than ever, we need to work together with relatives, neighbors and friends to leverage each other's strengths and skills to create opportunities for each other. I will show you how to create income from partnerships and understand problem-solving techniques in upcoming chapters. To avoid going broke starts with you thinking like an entrepreneur, then looking for problems to solve and opportunities to seize and maximize your position.

Question: What problem do people have in your city, church or job that you can solve and charge a reasonable fee?

2. **Adopt a "my money works for me" attitude**

People with money spend time figuring out how to get their money to work for them. When applied prudently and shrewdly, money can become a very diligent employee. Next time you make a budget; do your best to attach every dollar you plan to spend to an opportunity to get your money to return back to you or help advance your goals. For example, I will only consider buying a new pair of dress shoes if I have a paid speaking engagement. If you plan to upgrade your cell phone or purchase a laptop, for example, only do so if it's for business purposes. Make your money work for you; if you don't have a business need for the purchase then limit your spending only to personal needs, not wants.

> Money makes an excellent employee but a terrible boss. Make money work for you.

Question: Before making your next consumable purchase, decide if you can use the money as an investment into your future instead of making the purchase?

3.   Adopt a "I only borrow to my advantage" attitude

It is important to understand the difference between good debt and bad debt. Generally speaking, good debt creates than what it costs to pay back.People go into business because they want to make a profit. If the debt helps them do that, it's good debt. I suggest only taking loans earmarked for specific projects where you are confident it will generate income.

Bad debt is borrowing money for things that don't or can't produce a return. If the debt can't pay for itself, then it's bad debt. In other words, if the debt has to come from your personal income to pay the debt off, then it's considered to be bad debt. Borrow to your advantage. Your attitude towards personal debt, especially credit cards, should be to run the opposite way. A general rule of thumb is only borrow money if it's attached to a common sense business plan that will generate a consistent cash flow.

Question: Can you live with the principle: "if I don't have the money in the bank, then it's best to wait until I do, even if I am never in a position to buy it?"

4.   Adopt a "savers" attitude

People with a saver's attitude always have money and rarely go broke. These people buy off-the-rack clothes from modest retailers, drive used, cash purchased cars and rarely eat out. Yes, they are cheap. And most of them have what I call a "Take This Job and Shove It" fund accumulated to last them for 10 to 15 years should they leave their jobs. This fund comes from working 44 to 50 hours a week with a focused goal to save and invest, not spend.

On the other hand, most people with financial difficulties often suffer from *"detrimental consumption"* with high mortgaged house, high interest rate credit cards, at least one car note and designer labels in their closet. You may need to sell the golf clubs or host a yard sale to pay off debt. Develop a saver's attitude and turn your old stuff into cash and save money for your future.

Question: What things have you purchased that has now become a burden?

Question: Are you prepared emotionally to rid yourself of those things that have gotten you into debt?

5. **Adopt a "givers" attitude**
Although charitable giving dropped sharply among the wealthy after the 2000-2001 bear market, households with net worth of $5 million or more still gave away approximately 6% of their incomes. That compares to an average of about 2% overall and 4% for households with incomes under $25,000, according to American Demographics. Selfish stingy people who are only concerned about themselves will generally find themselves friendless and sometimes penniless.

God truly blesses those who give to the less fortunate. Givers realize they are blessed to be a blessing.

Question: Are you prepared to become one of the biggest givers in your city?

Question: What do you have in your life now that you can give away to help improve someone's company, idea or family?

Getting Rid of the Poverty Mentality

I lived in a community saturated with a poverty mentality. I grew up on the east side of Monroe, Michigan, where virtually everyone was either broke or part of the working poor. I would constantly hear family and friends use such negative, *poor mouth financial phrases* as:

- "I just got a new car financed for 5 years, this is my lucky day!"

- "One day I'm going to hit the lottery."

- "I'll always have a mortgage payment-- it is a fact of life."

- "You can't take it with you so you might as well spend it all now."

- "I am broke and probably will always be broke."

- "Some people are meant to be rich and other people are meant to be poor."

- "I'll never get ahead."

Poverty-minded people often pass on their adverse approach to life from one generation to the next. Instead of teaching the next generation the benefits of creating opportunities for themselves, saving for the future, launching new businesses, and developing income-producing assets, they unknowingly teach that "poverty will always be our lot in life unless someone gives us a handout."

A point of clarification here: *being poor minded has nothing to do with how much money is in your bank account.* Some wealthy people are living with a poverty mentality. Such people are generally stingy, lonely, bitter penny-pinchers who hoard their money because they live in fear of losing it. They define themselves by their possessions and fear they will lose their identity if they don't protect their wealth. Money is their god and the source of their happiness. Unfortunately, this mindset can be so destructive that if their possessions are taken away, they feel they have no reason to live.

Money, however, is a tool, a worker and a servant to you that should be used to advance your God-given talent, take care of your family and help others fulfill their destiny. Understanding the role of money in your life will help keep you from going broke.

After careful study of the more affluent in our society, I developed and then implemented a simple plan to not only avoid going broke but also begin providing for the future.

My "Avoid Going Broke" Plan

Your future will be here before you know it. But before you can begin to move toward your new status, you must get your financial house in order. The beauty of this simple six-step plan is you can begin today and start to see results in just a few months.

Step 1: Set up a Financial Game Plan Right Away

When my wife and I decided to build our home, we needed a $25,000 down payment in a relatively short period of time. In order to meet our deadline, we made a decision not to spend one penny on any unnecessary expenditure. We came up with a workable plan and held each other accountable until our goal was attained.

One very significant thing we did was look for ways to avoid impulse buying. For example, when we needed gas for our cars, we paid at the pump using a debit card. By not going into the convenient store we were not tempted to buy a can of soda or a candy bar. My wife came home one evening after work with chocolate on her breath. I asked her about it and she admitted spending ninety cents on a candy bar while at the gas station which proved to us the wisdom of this strategy. We accomplished our goal by planning our strategy together and holding each other accountable to the goal With daily and monthly goals, you can do the same. Set your goal and then develop a plan that is practical and achievable.

Step 2: Start Getting Out of Debt Immediately

The day that I became debt-free with no credit card, car or mortgage payment, my life dramatically changed for the better. Financial advisors will tell you the importance of becoming debt-free but seldom give you a practical way to do it.

Here is the strategy I used to become debt free:

> *First*, make up your mind not to create any new debt for at least two years. Set up a workable budget and stick to it. Two years is a small sacrifice to insure financial success in the future.

> *Next*, write down the monthly payment, interest rate, and total amount owed for each of your debts. Once you have your debts list, call each of your creditors and ask for a lower interest rate. Most credit card companies will work with you when you inform them you are working on a plan to pay the card off in full. Transfer your higher balances to cards with lower interest rate.

> *Finally*, use your savings to pay down your highest interest, non-tax deductible debt. It makes more sense to pay off debt at interest rates of 15% than to earn less than 2% interest in a money market or savings account. On all other debt, only pay the minimum until all higher interest rate debt is paid off. Then use the same methodology to eliminate the next highest debt and the next until all your debt is completely paid off.

Step 3: Save $1 a Day and Watch it Grow to $67,815

You can turn one dollar a day into $67,815 without a lot of effort or time. To start, take out the change in your pocket at the end of each day and drop it in a jar. You will discover it will average about $1 a day, which amounts to $7 a week and about $30 a month. This is money you've already paid taxes on in the form of withholding from your paycheck.

At the end of every month, deposit your $30 in a Roth IRA account, where it can grow tax-free and -- more important -- be withdrawn tax-free in the future. What's a measly $30 a month going to do for you? With a 10 percent annual return, your investment account will be worth $67,815 in a relatively short period of time. Not bad for pocket change, but that's just the beginning. I have listed below some other ideas:

Trim your expenses and begin to save even more

Activity	Monthly Savings	Annual Savings
Take-out vs. dining out once a month	$45	$540
Haircut and Manicure less often	$15	$180
Buy fewer bottles of water, drink tap water	$12	$144
Video rental vs. monthly movie in a theater	$11	$132
Regular coffee instead of cappuccino on weekdays	$40	$480
Total	**$123**	**$1,476**

If you can find $123 in your monthly budget, at a 10% interest rate it will grow to $278,040 in 30 years. You've financed half your retirement with just a few small sacrifices. As you begin to work this system, you will think of other ways to save small amounts that add up in a relatively short amount of time.

Step 4: Settle on the Right Motives

Most people end up in financial trouble because they have the wrong motives for making certain purchases. Learn how to be content with what you have and live below your current income level. That means do regular maintenances on your home and your car, being content   until you are debt free. Afterwards when you decide to make a major purchase; take the time to make wise financial decisions. Go through your closet determined to make due with what you have. Try creating new combinations from your current wardrobe.

Moving forward, before making any financial decision, ask yourself, "why?" Impressing your neighbors, college buddies or co-workers can lead to unnecessary debt that you will regret when the monthly bills come due.

Step 5: Stop Spending

Debt regret leads us to the next step toward getting out of debt which is to stop spending. The number one way to stop debt is to not create any new debt. Go on a spending "fast" for the next few months. That means each month absolutely no unnecessary spending. Your discretionary or extra income can be surprising. These funds can be used as a great jump start for eradicating your current debt.   Never shop without a list and commit your spending to the list. If you or your mate tends to impulse buy, agree to shop together and hold each other accountable. Make sure you know the boundaries before you walk into any store of any kind. Never shop when you're hungry, avoid looking through "sale ads" and never go window shopping.

Step 6: Stay With The Car You Have

The most common errors made when car buying are purchasing more car than we need, financing it for too long, and trading it too soon. If you're constantly broke and can't figure out why, the answer may be sitting in your driveway. Americans may not be buying as many vehicles as in the past, but the *way* we buy our cars is detrimental to the average family budget.

According to Liz Weston, a certified financial planner and columnist on the MSN Money website, we get in trouble buying cars because of the way we borrow or finance them. Here are three reasons people get in over their heads when buying cars and three solutions to get it right the next time you are in the market.

> **Problem:** *Financing a new car for four or more years*
> **Solution:** *Learn the difference between needs and wants*

We all need to get to the grocery store and to work but not one of us "needs" a brand new car. I would recommend avoiding a car loan.   Purchase a reliable used or pre-owned vehicle. Empty your savings account or take public transportation until you save enough to pay cash and avoid a car loan. Avoid long-term debt for a vehicle; especially a new car. Automobiles depreciate in value as soon as you drive them off the car lot. You may want a new car but you do not need one! Use some of the money you will save in interest to have a reliable mechanic inspect the used car you think will meet your family's needs.

➢ **Problem:** *Rolling debt from one car to another*
Solution: *Keep the car you have longer by faithful maintenance.*

Today's cars are better built and more dependable than ever. This means that unless you've got a real lemon you could keep it passed 200,000 or even 300,000 miles. I have driven several cars well passed the 200,000 mile mark. My brother-in-law drove his family car passed 400,000 miles. His secret: consistent and regular oil changes (every 3,000 to 4,000 miles). There's no requirement that says you must trade or sell a car because of a certain mileage.

➢ **Problem:** *You owe more on the car than it's worth.*
Solution: *Look at the Overall Costs.*

When purchasing a car, most people only look at the monthly payment. You also need to factor in insurance, gas, maintenance, repairs, sales tax, and depreciation. Most cars will set you back at least *twice* the initial purchase price over the next five years.

The Plan Works!

With two young daughters and a mortgage that was becoming difficult to pay, my friends Jack and his stay-at-home wife Laura, needed a plan to avoid going broke on a $31,000 a year teacher's salary. The ever increasing financial pressure put a serious strain on their marriage. Initially Jack considered taking a second job at night to help make ends meet. As they discussed possible options and considered the positive and negative consequences of each one, they realized they needed a financial game plan or they might lose everything.

The first step of their plan was to find a more reasonably priced house and sell their existing home. This was not an easy decision for them. They were married and gave birth to their two beautiful daughters in that house. They discovered that the emotional attachment of family memories and holiday celebrations was holding them back from seeking a more affordable mortgage. They chose to look toward the future rather than live in the past. They sat down at the kitchen table together and calmly wrote down a financial plan. The initial goals in the new plan:

1. Get out of debt
2. Stop all impulse spending
3. Save 20 percent of every dollar that came into their hands.

After several months, Jack and Laura found a more affordable home and sold their existing one. The next adjustment to their spending motives produced additional savings also. Instead of buying new furniture and a new car with the profits of their sale, they put six months of living expenses into an interest bearing saving account.

> For most people, their financial woes are not income issues, it's bad money management over the money they do have.

By making a few wise financial decisions, they are now living comfortably and making new memories by taking at least one family vacation each year. They are living free from personal debt and Jack can continue doing what he enjoys and is gifted to do; teach. Laura can enjoy being home with the children as they live very comfortably within their means.

Jack excitedly shares that they no longer worry about losing their home or going broke, even in this unstable economy. They are a living testimony of how easy it is to avoid going broke using a simple practical financial game plan.

You're On Your Way!

Now that you have the basics you can begin your journey to financial success, wealth and prosperity. Take the time to review this chapter's powerful financial principles and do the practical applications suggested below in the chapter principles. You can begin to build your life around your plan, the goals you have set rather than worrying about how you are going to pay next month's bills.

I believe you are now ready for the next level of your financial freedom. Check yourself. Take my brief financial test and review the practical application check list on the next page to ensure you have all the required tools to get out of debt and help you stay out of debt forever.

Chapter Principles
My Personal Challenges to You

1. Being broke is a temporary condition and if you are willing to educate yourself financially, then your financial condition can significantly improve.

   Do you want to improve your financial condition? _____
   What are your plans to continue your financial education?
   _____
   _____

2. You can pass a wealth or a poverty mindset on to the next generation.

   Which do you choose to pass on to your next generation?
   _____
   How do you plan to pass on a wealthy-mindset to your family?
   _____
   _____

3. Being poor-minded has nothing to do with how much money is in your bank account.

   How do you feel about your present financial condition?
   _____

4. Learn how to be content with your current income level, where you live, what you drive and what your wear.

   Can you agree to implement this principle in your life?
   _____

_____

5. Most of us have a shot at being a millionaire even in this down economy.

   Do you want to take a shot at being a millionaire?

   _____

6. The number one way to stop debt is to not create any new debt. Do you agree? _____

7. Many people end up in financial trouble because they have the wrong motives and/or information for making certain purchases.

   Are you prepared to stop using credit cards and impulse buying?

   _____

Practical Application:

If you have not already done so, review the explanation of my simple six-step plan. Check each one off as you implement it in your life. Start making your money work for you.

- ☐ Set up a financial game plan
- ☐ Start getting out of debt
- ☐ Save $1 a day, deposit monthly
- ☐ Settle on right motives
- ☐ Stop Impulsive/Unplanned Spending
- ☐ Stay with the car you have

Life Changing Answers Available in This Chapter

➤ How can I determine my life's purpose and talents?

➤ What's in my DNA that can help me financially prosper?

➤ How do I get back on track if I've not built my life on purpose?

Chapter 2

BUILD YOUR LIFE ON PURPOSE

Your financial success is in your DNA.

I mentioned in the first chapter that I grew up in a community where a poverty mentality was the norm rather than the exception. I want to take the time to share with you how I overcame that the poverty influence on my life and moved into a prosperous and fruitful lifestyle. I believe by sharing my story and the struggles I overcame, you will see that the plans and solutions I present in this book come out of my own experiences. I learned many of these lessons the hard way but you can learn from my mistakes. If I was able to rise above my circumstances and become a person of purpose and wealth, so can you.

Desperate for a Paycheck

My wife was pregnant with our first daughter, a new house with an overwhelming mortgage, and two hefty car payments when I suddenly found myself unemployed. I had a college degree and years of professional sales experience yet I was nearly broke with very little hope of getting out of my negative financial situation. I was so desperate for a job and a paycheck I even applied at a local gas station. They were not hiring and my desperation deepened as I learned firsthand how hard it was to live without a steady income.

I wandered from one temporary job to the next and lived paycheck to paycheck without any real financial stability. On top of that I was never content working for someone else even when I did manage to bring home a meager paycheck. There was always a persistent ache in my heart that yearned for something more than a job. I knew this was not the way I wanted to spend the rest of my life. I began to look around for people who seemed successful in the business world and studied their history. Those that rose from nothing to millionaire were of particular interest to me. If they could do it, shouldn't I be able to as well?

I implemented the steps I presented to you in the first chapter then I began to dig deeper into things successful people did differently than me. Obviously they were not living from paycheck to paycheck like I had been doing. They had learned a secret to life that I had not yet discovered. What I found may surprise you. My struggles came because I did not understand a very important aspect of my life; my *raison d'être*.

The Master Key to Your Success

Raison d'être is a phrase borrowed from the French which means, "reason for being." Your *raison d'être* is your purpose in life, the reason you were born. What I discovered is not only do I have a *raison d'être* but also unique God-given talents and skills designed to help me accomplish that specific purpose. Like most people, I realize I spent too much time trying to emulate others as I sought to uncover my own identity. Now I understand an original is always more valuable than a copy or a fake.

Trying to be like other people actually prevented me from discovering my specific *raison d'être*. My life was plagued by questions leaving me virtually paralyzed with insecurity. Who am I? Why was I born? What are my God-given talents? The day I discovered my *raison d'être* and focused on my God-given gifts, skills and talents I stopped chasing a paycheck and pursed my reason for being.

Knowing my *raison d'être* gave my life meaning and allowed me to stop fulfilling other people's purposes and focus on mine. I learned to live life setting goals and priorities that moved me toward accomplishing my purpose in life. I no longer felt insignificant, unappreciated, underpaid and disappointed with my life. I

> An original is always more valuable than a copy or a fake. What the world needs from you is authenticity.

want to help you discover your *raison d'être* and show you how to unlock your God-given talents. You can begin to build your life on purpose instead of merely working for a paycheck and fulfilling someone else's *raison d'être*.

Raison d'être : It's In Your DNA

Programmed within your human genetic code is a unique set of divine rules. Molecular biologist Hargobind Khorana received the Nobel Peace Prize in 1968 for his work on the interpretation of this unique genetic code. He found embedded within our DNA, living cells which are responsible for our personality, eye color, blood type and other physical characteristics. More importantly, our DNA has also been encoded with a divine *raison d'être* that is perfectly tailored-made for each individual human being. Once you discover your pre-programmed *raison d'être* and set your life on a path that cooperates with rather than fights against your unique code, your life will become easier!

According to Dr. Zorda Pastor, a professor at the University of Wisconsin Medical School, people living in line with their purpose lead healthier lives and ultimately create more financial opportunities for themselves than those that don't. She also discovered that those who follow their pre-programmed *raison d'être* typically don't retire. They merely continue to enjoy life doing what they were designed and equipped to do. People who make excuses for being unhappy, unfilled or unsuccessful are most likely not on the path toward fulfilling their personal *raison d'être*.

I discovered a profound yet simple secret that changed my life and has continually moved me forward with confidence and purpose. Seeking money and physical possessions before seeking your *raison d'être* leads to a dissatisfaction with life. I recently met with a billionaire who earns his money in the technology industry and employs over 4,000 people. As we sat down in his office, I thought our meeting was about how I could assist with his business growth. We discovered he was spending his time and running his business without purpose. Even though he had lots of nice things and was living a very comfortable lifestyle, he desired something else; he needed to fulfill his true *raison d'être*.

> Life becomes easier when you cooperate with your *raison d'être* rather than fight against it.

Why Seek and Develop Raison d'être

People who understand their *raison d'être* act and speak with clear purpose and direction. The most frustrated person in the world is someone who has a dream but doesn't have the money, the know-how, the influence, or the relationships to make it happen. When people are aimlessly wandering through life and wasting their divine potential, they severely limit themselves and seldom find peace. There are many benefits to diligently seeking your *raison d'être*. Three very beneficial economic reasons are:

1. Pursuit of your *raison d'être* is the only way to guarantee true success in life.
2. Living within your true *raison d'être* brings out your God-given uniqueness.
3. Understanding your *raison d'être clar*ifies where and how you should spend your most precious commodity; your time.

Success Guaranteed

Many people don't immediately recognize their gifts because they seem so natural. The mistaken mindset believes we must earn a living by the sweat of our brow. This misguided thinking contributes to overlooking what should be obvious. When people say, "Oh, you are so good at this or that," we normally dismiss what is actually a very profound observation on their part. What comes easy and gets complimented by others may be a clue to your specific purpose. Instead of working hard and despising your mundane daily routine, why not enjoy your work and feel a sense of accomplishment at the end of each day. Sound impossible?

> The most frustrated person in the world is someone who has a dream but doesn't have the money and the relationships to make it happen.

A woman named Dottie Wilcox loved to bake cakes and found that sharing a slice of cake with neighbors and friends made them smile. She took slices of cake to friends at work during their lunch break. She willingly gave free slices of cake to anyone who asked. Her slices of cakes became so popular among the workers that she charged a small fee to keep up with the requests. In 1993 she launched her company, "A Piece of Cake," that now ships cakes all around the world. She makes millions of dollars doing what she loves.

Wally Amos, founder of "Famous Amos Cookies," followed a similar pattern. He started baking cookies for friends as thank you gifts. He had so many orders, that he had to start a company just to meet the demand. Neither Wally Amos nor Dottie Wilcox sat down and thought, "I will be a cookie or a cake maker." They simply walked a path using their gifts to make others happy and that path lead to financial success. They found their purpose in life by doing something they loved and giving to others.

> The reason you are not comfortable being an unknown cog turning the wheels in someone else's company is because you were not born to fit another's purpose.

Each of us has specific gifts, talents and skills but they come with a responsibility to develop and use them to their fullest potential. We will still work hard but we are more satisfied with the results of our efforts and have a more positive outlook on life. It starts with you being active doing something you already love to do.

You Are Naturally Unique by Design

In economics, the value of a thing is determined by how rare and unique it is. When you buy a diamond, it is expensive because no two diamonds are alike. Gold is costly because it is difficult to find. Real pearls are expensive because they are rare; found only in a small number of mollusks. Oil is expensive because it doesn't just spring up in your backyard; you generally have to dig deep for it.

If you shop at a discount clothing store, you'll notice that many of the ties, coats, shirts and pants are just alike, varying only in size. They are inexpensive because they were mass produced. If you want an original, you need to work with a designer to create a garment that will fit your body and personality perfectly. Of course an original is more expensive and valuable.

You are an original, uniquely custom-made by The Master Designer. There is no one else quite like you anywhere in the universe. The reason you are not comfortable being an unknown cog turning the wheels in someone else's company is because you were not born to blend in and conform to fit someone else's purpose. You may start your career on an assembly line but you were never meant to live life on a sales rack.

The sooner you discover your *raison d'être,* and define your unique gifts and talents, the quicker you will get on the path to success and fulfillment. The more you express and market your true personal talents, gifts and skills, the more you will be in demand.

> The more you express, market and promote your *raison d'être* the more you will be in demand.

If you try to fit into another's definition of who you are to satisfy them, the best you will ever be is number two. Like precious metals or oil, your uniqueness is buried deep in your heart. Your ideas become more original the deeper you dig. Your original ideas increase your income potential and personal satisfaction.

Time Wasters and Energy Drainers

Living in line with your *raison d'être* will help you eliminate time wasters and avoid energy drainers. Your most precious commodity is your time, where and how you spend it is of the utmost importance. You must value your time if you really want to move ahead in life. It is a deeply distressing fact that while we all have been given unique gifts and talents, too often we ignore them by engaging in time-consuming irrelevant activities. We waste precious time when we focus our energy on anything but accomplishing our true *raison d'être.*

If pleasing people is the center focus of your life, you will never fulfill your *raison d'être.* If you are depend on someone else to discover and help you fulfill your *raison d'être,* you'll always be undervalued and often underpaid. I only spend my precious time and energy on things where my God-given gifts and talents can be expressed and further developed. Activities outside your *raison d'être are* time-wasters and energy-drainers. Until you discover your purpose in life and identify your unique gifts and talents, you are vulnerable to everyone else's ideas about you. Don't waste any more of your precious time draining all your energy saddled with misconceptions and a wrong self-perspective and ; striving to fulfill someone else's *raison d'être.*

Myths and Clues About Your *Raison d'être*

Let's deal with six prominent myths that can keep you from realizing your true *raison d'être.* After each myth, carefully consider the questions and look for clues to help you uncover your life's purpose.

Myth #1: "My *raison d'être* must be something I don't like to do."

Your *raison d'être* is tied to your passions and interests. The gifts, talents and skills to accomplish your purpose are things you already like doing. Depending on the length of time you've been influenced by this myth, you may have to dig deep within yourself to discover your true passions. A passion is something close to your heart and that you enjoy doing. As you begin this search, be careful not to take on another's *raison d'être.* Only you can really determine your true passions.

Clues to uncovering your raison d'être:

- What are you most passionate about?

- What problems in the world would you like to see solved?

- If money was not an issue, what would you be doing with your life?

- What angers you the most in the world today?

- What could you do to change the things that anger you?

Myth #2: "My job is my *raison d'être*."

Your job is definitely not your *raison d'être*. With over 2.6 million U.S. jobs lost in 2009, the average person can now expect to have four to six different jobs during their lifetime. If your current job is your raison d'être, what happens to your sense of purpose when your job changes? People who place their identity in their employment are likely to suffer from anxiety and find it difficult to enjoy days off or vacations because of the fear this myth breeds.

Clues to uncovering your raison d'être:

- Beyond the education and qualifications listed on your resume, why did your past or current employer hire you?

- What did your employer see in you that made him choose you over other applicants?

- What skills have you developed on your current job?

- What do you normally think about during your off-hours?

Myth #3: "My role is my raison d'être."

If you ask people "who" they are, most will tell you "what" they do. Men tend to define themselves in terms of what they do professionally instead of their purpose in life. "I am an accountant." "I am a sales consultant." Women generally define their *raison d'être* in terms of their relationships or roles such as mother or wife. Allowing your profession or role to define your *raison d'être* puts you in a very precarious position. If you lose your job or your role changes through death or divorce, what does that do to your purpose in life? Your *raison d'être* is always bigger than your current role, relationship or job title.

Clues to uncovering your raison d'être:

- What do other people say that you do exceptionally well?

- When you were a teenager, what did you imagine doing with your life?

- In what ways can you use your current role, relationship or job title to develop your talents and skills?

Myth #4: "My raison d'être is my college major."

Your *raison d'être* may not have anything to do with your college major. According to Dr. Robert Pitcher, a professor at the University of Alabama's Center for Teaching and Learning, cites that every year more than 380,000 students fail college in the United States. The impact of college failure can cause lasting damage to self-esteem, which can influence an entire lifetime of choices. In my opinion, this alarming statistic is the result of belief in a myth. Knowledge is the key to success. Moreover, those students who do graduate often spend their next five to ten years working in non-career related jobs to pay off their huge college debt. Most students rarely work in their field of study..

42

Knowledge is not the key to success. Wisdom, which is the ability to use knowledge, is the only way to succeed in life. If you don't know how to use the knowledge that you have acquired, then that knowledge is useless. College is not a bad thing but your time and money should be spent pursuing and developing your God-given gifts and talents.

Clues to uncovering your raison d'être:

- How can you use what you learned in school to move you closer to following your true passion?

- What subjects and experiences at school excited you the most?

Myth #5: "My raison d'être has to have a global impact."

At first glance, this myth might sound very noble but it may in fact discourage many from pursuing their true purpose in life. Your God-given talents may someday lead to alleviating world hunger but no matter how big your vision, you will have to start out helping people in your direct sphere of influence. Your neighborhood, your workplace, your child's school and your local community are where you begin to develop and grow the talents and skills that will lead you to discover your true *raison d'être*. Many highly successful entrepreneurs, like Sam Walton of Wal-Mart, started by helping other people. He simply wanted to help people live simpler lives.

Clues to uncovering your raison d'être:

- What small acts of kindness do you enjoy doing for others?

- What group of people do you believe you can help the most?

- What problems do you see around your neighborhood or city that you can help solve?

Myth #6: "My birth was an accident."

God doesn't make mistakes and no birth is ever accidental. Everyone has a divine *raison d'être* and the God-given talents to accomplish it. Everyone and everything in the earth has a distinct reason for being. Look around you. Trees are producing oxygen so humans can breathe. Scientist and physicists agree that even a seemingly insignificant event such as a butterfly flapping its wings in Africa can affect the atmosphere in Alaska. Imagine every word we speak and every action we take has an effect on the world. Regardless of your circumstances, you were birthed to make an impact in this world. You were born for a specific reason.

Clues to uncovering your raison d'être:

- Has anyone ever told you your birth was an accident?

- How do you feel about that now?

- Do you believe there is a plan and purpose for your life?

- What have you discovered about your *raison d'être?*

- What have you learned about your God-given gifts, talents and skills?

Getting Back on Track

The only reason we fail is we have lost focus and gotten off course. Myths, traditions, out-dated practices and false mindsets passed through the generations have distracted many of us from uncovering our true purpose for life. Dealing with life without a purpose causes us to make decisions that could take us down the wrong path. Now that you are more aware of your *raison d'être,* you need to learn to make life decisions that continually move you closer to fulfilling your true purpose.

We move off-track in life when we make decisions based on feelings, circumstances or a promotion instead of taking the time to understand if this option helps fulfill our *raison d'être*. It is crucial that we begin to make deliberate calculated decisions based on principles and direction--our lives depend on it. God has given us talent and the skills to get to our prescribed destination.

Decisions based on feelings and circumstances tend to lead us astray.

I know people who became involved in a network marketing company after attending a charismatic and exciting business presentation. After joining the organization they realized the decision was based on emotional excitement and shallow promises of riches. Life decisions should be based on accomplishing our *raison d'être* and utilizing our God-given talents, not an emotional whim or marketing hype.

Deciding to accept a job or promotion because it looks good without carefully comparing it to our true *raison d'être* may lead us away from accomplishing our true purpose in life.

Some years ago, I worked as a district manager for a successful consulting firm. I quickly produced record sales and caught the attention of the company's senior vice-president. He offered me a promotion with substantial financial benefits but it meant moving my family from Atlanta, Georgia to Tampa, Florida. My wife and I compared the benefits and hardships this move could bring on our family. Then we carefully considered whether Tampa, Fl would place us closer to our *raison d'être.* I turned down the promotion still experienced increased business opportunities. Staying true to your *raison d'être* will produce a life-time of rewards.

We invest time and money in other people's dreams rather than in accomplishing our own *raison d'être.*

You are responsible for developing your God-given talents so you can fulfill your purpose in life. Like a professional athlete, you must invest your time, money and energy in perfecting your unique set of skills. If you stay on focus and know where you are going, when the right opportunities come along you will be ready, willing and able to move into them. Competing in a sports event that you have not properly planned and trained for is extremely dangerous. The same is true in the financial world. Investing without taking the time to develop your skills could bring devastating financial consequences. It's time to invest in you.

Entering into a relationship or partnership with someone whose raison d'être is contrary to yours can become a hindrance to both parties.

Every relationship, whether it is professional or personal, should ensure both parties increase their God-given talents and continually move forward toward their individual *raison d'être.* If we don't realize the importance of our relationships in accomplishing our personal purposes, we will compromise and suppress our individual potential and life purpose.

Let Go of Whatever Makes You Stop

If you are intelligent but not developing your God-given talents, people may reward your intellect for to fulfill a need; but your contentment lies in striving for your potential. If you are educated but don't understand your *raison d'être*, you'll end up depressed, frustrated and tired. Regardless of how much money you make, you'll find no real happiness or satisfaction in life without obstacles to conquer and goals to achieve. Overcoming obstacles and achieving goals are your checklist for progress. Are you moving forward or stuck in a rut? I like what John Mason writes in his book, *Let Go of Whatever Makes You Stop*. People say they want riches but what they really need is a fulfillment of purpose. Life satisfaction only comes when we focus on accomplishing our individual purpose.

> People say they want riches but what they really need is fulfillment of purpose.

There are those who believe in fate but fate is uncertain and cannot be controlled or understood. Highly successful people are motivated by a dynamic purpose and seize each moment as an opportunity. They wait on or hope for fate to present an opportunity. Highly successfully people focused on being prepared for every opportunity. Once you discover your *raison d'être*, begin developing your unique God-given talents and strive to line your life up according to your true purpose, you'll begin to see a bright new future unfolding before you. Build your life on purpose using the tools God has given you and stop living your life around a job.

As you get your life back on the right track, you will find you won't have to chase after money; your *raison d'être* will put you in demand. Wealth will begin to follow you.

Chapter Principles
And My Personal Challenges to You

1. People living in line with their *raison d'être* live longer, lead healthier lives and ultimately create more financial opportunities for themselves.

   Are you living in line with your *raison d'être?* _____

   What decision do you need to make to put your life on your *raison d'être* path? _____

2. Without understanding personal *raison d'être*, one may acquire nice things and live a fairly comfortable life, but there will always be a longing for "something else."

   Do you long for that "something else"? _____

   Define what you believe that "something else" is.
   _____

3. The reason people fail is because they've lost focus of their personal *raison d'être*.

   Have you ever felt like a failure? _____

4. Regardless of how much money you make, you'll not find real happiness without a personal *raison d'être* to accomplish.

   Are you on course toward accomplishing your *raison d'être?*
   _____

_____

5. Your job is not your *raison d'être*.

Does your current job utilize your God-given talents, gifts and skills? _____.

How can you use your job to enhance your *raison d'etre*.

6. The greatest misfortune in a person's life is not death, but a life lived without purpose.
Are you living your life on purpose or someone else's ideas?
_____

Practical Application:

1.   Circle the words below that accurately describe your current job.

Lackluster	Invigorating	Boring
Fulfilling	Dead-end	Stimulating
Stressful	Exhausting	Energizing
Useless	Worthwhile	Secure
Rewarding	Humiliating	Fun

2.   Your *raison d'être* fits you and your personality perfectly.

Circle the words or phrases that best describe you and your personality.

Extravert	Introvert	Shy
Outgoing	Serious	Fun-loving
Quiet	Spontaneous	Practical
Imaginative	Objective	Easy-going
Logical	Sentimental	Visionary

3.   Your **raison d'être** is something that you like doing and is tied to your passion and your interests. List three things you really enjoy doing.

_____   _____

_____

4.   One of the reasons many of us don't recognize our God-given gifts is because they seem so natural to us. What God-given gifts have you discovered you have?

_____   _____

_____

5.   What were you born to do with your life?

_____

If you are still not sure, review the section on Myths and Clues.

<u>NOTES</u>

Life Changing Answers Available in This Chapter

1. How can my new habits save me $20,000 each year?

2. How can I improve my cash flow?

3. What are ways to boost my income today?

Chapter 3

DEVELOP HEALTHY FINANCIAL HABITS

Financial success is never an accident.

A bad financial habit is like picking up a cigarette for the first time as a kid. Someone in your life told you that smoking could lead to an addiction and ultimately kill you. Perhaps you wanted to try smoking anyway; because as a child you thought that you would live forever and never get sick.

Financially speaking, some of us get addicted to emotional overspending or we neglect/re budgeting because we believe these habits contribute to financial collapse. If a person smoked cigarettes consistently for 5, 10 or 20 years, his or her health would certainly decline. Doctors agree that good health in future must begin with kicking the bad habits and starting good ones now. Just as a person must develop smart eating and exercise habits to stay physically fit, one must develop good financial habits to stay financially fit.

Financial success is never an accident. To become financially stable, our habits must be intentional, deliberate and calculated.

Unfortunately, my financial habits included impulsive spending, unbalanced checkbooks, and mismanagement of income. I discovered my financial dilemmas were not related to income- but money management.. My financial habits were leading me to the poor-house.

To begin to make the important transition from a paycheck-seeking life to a purpose-seeking life, it is important we develop good financial habits so that we save enough money to retire strong and leave a lasting legacy for our families.

How To Save $20,000

There are many ways you can save money and still have an active life without living like a miser. I like nice cars, clothes and dining with friends at nice restaurants. I certainly enjoy family vacations each year and attending sporting events.

As you discipline yourself to reach your financial goals, here are a few smart ways you can save over $20,000 in the next 12 months and still

> You are never too broke or too rich to save money.

enjoy quality entertainment, eat well and look good, even with a modest income.

1. **Take hotel-free vacations**
    Our friends, Robert and Dianne, take hotel-free vacations through a new opportunity called home exchanging. There are websites and companies that will connect you with a house in the city and state of your destination. In exchange, you register your home, typically for free, with their website. If you live in Boston, for example, and want to vacation in southern California, a home exchange company will find a family wanting to travel from southern California to the New England area. You exchange your home for the week for theirs. Depending upon the number of family vacations you take a year, you could save thousands of dollars in hotel and restaurant cost.

Annual vacations costs savings: **Approximately: $2,000**

2. Get important articles and news on line for free

I used to have four newspapers and three magazines delivered to my home and office. Now everyone can read virtually every major publication on line each morning for free. Most media outlets haven't figured out how to monetize their publications on the internet, so currently, the majority of their information and articles are free.

Annual Newspaper and Magazine savings: **$360**.

3. Exercise at home

You can work out anywhere for free. (i.e. jog or bike in your neighborhood, do sit ups in your living room, do pushups in your bedroom or do aerobics with a DVD) I've had costly memberships that were a total waste of money. Even when I didn't use the membership, I still got charged for the entire year. I get a lot of exercise, but I do it at home and on the road. You can workout at home and stay in the best shape of your life.

Approximate Fitness Membership 35/month: **Annual savings: $420**.

4. Watch recorded programming

Instead of paying expensive monthly cable bills, try watching DVDs, or reading a book a month (you can save a lot of money purchasing used books and movies at most popular movie and book stores). If you are like me, I don't spend much money buying DVDs since I rarely watch a movie more than once. Rentals are more cost effective entertainment for me.

Approximate cable costs $65/month. **Annual savings: $780**.

5. Discover free leisure activities

I don't go to clubs, or the theater, or ballet, or opera or professional sporting events. If meeting people is important to you or your career, there are other ways to be sociable and have fun while taking care of business. There are plenty of networking meetings around your city where the host organization pays for the facility and refreshments.

Approximate leisure activity cost $120/month: **Annual savings: $1,200.**

6. Live a healthy lifestyle.

If you smoke cigarettes, drink soda or coffee on a daily basis or perhaps drink alcohol, it could cost you a minimum of $5 per day. We won't count the ensuing health care expenses that this lifestyle will cost you in the near future.

Unhealthy living costs at $5 per day: **Annual savings: $1,825**

7. Go on a year-long spending fast

Going to the mall is a favorite pastime for most people. The food court alone costs $30 for two people, and if you bought the 25% of stuff that I "want" would be another $25-75. Cha-ching. I try my best to avoid the mall and only go when I absolutely need something, which is very rare. Most of consumables, like household items, shaving cream and necessities can come from discount stores. Understand the difference from your "needs" and your "wants". It'll save you tremendously.

Avoidable shopping: **Annual savings: Approximately$2,600.**

8. Rarely go to the movies

I used to go to the movies two to three monthly. Since makinng a decision to massively save money, I realized rarely is a movie "must see" the weekend it hits the theatre. I can wait until it comes out on DVD or pay-per-view where my entire family can watch the movie at home for one low price. As of this writing, the average adult movie ticket is now in the United State is $10 which increases to $20-$25 when you include concessions. Now we take the kids to the park or out to do something more fun and creative. This saves as least $50 per month, although it's more if we factored in the costs of my kids' tickets, and concessions.

Going out to movies consistently: **Annual saving: $600**

9. Have only one paid-for car

As I wrote extensively in Chapter 1, many people's financial woes begin with a car. Too much car, financed too long, traded too soon. If you're constantly broke and can't figure out why, the answer may be sitting in your driveway. Americans may not be buying as many vehicles as we did in the past, but the way we buy is certainly hurting the average family -- and it's driving some to the breaking point. If you have at least one paid for car and it runs well, keep it maintained.

Paid for car: **Annual saving: perhaps $5,000**

10. Brown bag it

Many people who work outside their home eat out every day, at a cost of $8-20 per lunch. I would suggest bringing leftovers or a sandwich, fruits, pretzels and snacks. This lunch costs less than $5.

Brown Bagging it: **Annual savings: $2,600**.

11. Buy clothes and household items at consignment shops

Many retailers and manufacturers are now selling their products through consignment shops giving consumers big discounts. A consignment shop is a second hand or used product store offering items at a lower cost. To remove the stigma of buying "used stuff", there is normally a quality and standards test these items must pass to be sold in this market. You can buy high quality athletic equipment, men's clothing, women's suits, children's clothing, tools, toys, furniture, automobiles and books. One of the bright spots in our economy is the rise of consignment shops.

Year-long shopping at consignment shops rather than retail: **Annual savings: Approximately $2,000**

12. No more expensive coffees or snacks

I used to buy either a smoothie, bottled water or a latte every day. At a cost of about $4 per latte, sometimes I'd get two. Now, we make our own smoothies and coffee

Annual savings: Approximately $1,000.

Your spending maybe more or less than listed above (depending on the size of your family), but you can still find a savings even on a modest income. Your financial goals should be based on keeping as much money in your bank account as possible. Increasing your wealth begins with you massively saving all you can, paying down debt and becoming an excellent manager over your income.

Total Savings: $20,385!
Your retirement fund just became healthier!

Avoid The Big 5

Five bad financial habits you must avoid

In the past, you might have been able to count on raises at work and a gradually improving standard of living to bail you out. But those doors are closing for many because:

> Incomes aren't growing as they did in the past. In fact, the Census Bureau stats when adjusted for inflation, median incomes are below where they were in 1999.

- Inflation and health care costs chew up a bigger part of what we earn.

These setbacks can easily send you over the financial edge into bankruptcy; especially when you are in the midst of financial struggles. With so many issues attacking your financial stability, it is important that you understand the basics of financial management.

To ensure you have the right approach to money, I have provided the 5 Bad Habits to Avoid and my advice to help you stay financially healthy.

1. **Not Knowing Where Your Money Goes**
   If you're broke, you need to find out where every nickel is being spent so you can make intelligent decisions about how to trim. A friend of mine, thatdug his way out of $35,000 in debt, says getting a handle on his spending helped him turn around his finances.

   Robert's advice: Technology makes that easier than ever before to help you get out of debt. You can use personal-finance software such as Money or Quicken, or sign up for an online solution like Mint, Wesabe, Yodlee or Quicken Online. Invest into one of these software products today. They are worth the money.

2. **Confusing needs and wants**

This is a major issue for people at every income level. However, when you are struggling financially, **the consequences of** deciding you *need* something that's actually a *want* can be devastating.

Our needs are few, and they include shelter, food, clothes, transportation and companionship. Our wants are endless and quickly will transform a need like transportation (which can be a $5,000 used car) into an extravagance such as a new luxury sports car.

Robert's advice: To help get your finances under control, write down what you really need, and how to get it for less. If you find yourself saying, "I need a (whatever)," stop a moment and consider whether you really do. You probably don't have to live without it forever -- just long enough to truly get on your feet.

3. **Buying Big Stuff The Wrong Way**

A lot of "save money" advice focuses on the little stuff such as how to cut back on lattes or trim your utility bill by a few bucks. But those who are chronically short of cash often overspend on the big stuff, especially shelter and transportation.

Robert's advice: If your mortgage or rent payment eats up much more than 30% of your gross income or your vehicle costs you more than 10% (including financing, repairs and gas), you're going to have a tough time making ends meet. Call and write your lenders immediately to negotiate a lower rate. Continue to call until you get results. If your lender is unwilling to work with you on the rate, consider selling it for a more affordable option. Riding in a car that's eating up your retirement funds is no way to live.

4. **Only Considering the Monthly Payment Amount**
   Whole businesses thrive on getting you to ignore the total cost of your purchase. Payday lenders, rent-to-own shops and car dealerships want you to focus on the short-term payments, not the long-term expense. Stay away from payday lenders and rent-to-own shops.

   Robert's advice: Anytime you consider a loan, bring a calculator so you can multiply payments by the number of months you'll be on the hook to get the real cost of what you're buying.

5. **Living Paycheck To Paycheck**
   Every setback is a crisis when you have no cushion. Failing to have any savings also increases the chances you'll bounce checks, incurring expensive fees. You will likely pay bills late, which means more fees as you trash your credit scores. Credit scores are those all-important numbers that determine how much you pay for loans, insurance and housing.

   Robert's advice: A couple of hundred dollars can make a difference. Always ensure you have at least $500 in the bank for emergencies and cushion by saving every cent you can.

Habits That Will Improve Cash Flow

If your budget is like that of so many other households, it may seem like you never have quite enough cash on hand to pay all your bills. At the end of every month there is nothing to set aside for a rainy day. And these days, your cash crunch may be worse than ever if your expenses are rising, your income is falling and your credit limits are diminishing.

Though there aren't really any new ideas in cash management, here are *six tried-and-true techniques* that can help you improve your liquidity and boost your cash flow. You don't have to resort to drastic measures like selling your home, bailing out of your long-term investments or even raiding your jewelry box.

1. Earn more interest

One way to improve your monthly cash position is to transfer extra cash in your checking account into higher yield investments such as short-term CDs or money market funds. Even a savings account could be a smart move if you have any cash that's not earning some sort of return, however small the amount may be.

The downside is that these types of investments are "sort of a losing game" because they rarely earn a high enough return to overcome inflation. Worse yet, bank fees can wipe out or exceed any interest you earn on a checking or savings account. If you have multiple accounts that are dinged to the tune of $10 or $12 every month, you might want to reduce those costs by consolidating your cash into fewer accounts. Don't exceed the Federal Deposit Insurance Corp., or FDIC, limit of $250,000 in any one account.

2. Get rate cuts

Again, ask your credit card company for a lower rate. And, ask again if they decline you. A lower rate will make a difference in your monthly cash flow. Either way, lower finance charges will reduce your monthly costs, improve your cash flow and help you pay off your debt sooner. Be cautious about balance-transfer offers: Some credit cards have high fees that outweigh the benefit of a lower interest rate.

If your cash crunch is due to unaffordable mortgage payments, you might be able to refinance your loan. The federal government and some states offer attractive foreclosure-prevention financing for people who are overextended and meet the qualifications.

3. Tap your equity

Sometimes, a severe cash shortage that can't be ameliorated by spending cuts or investment reallocations may necessitate some type of short-term debt to resolve. If you know how to handle personal credit and are disciplined, planners generally suggest a home equity line of credit first, followed by a retirement account loan and then credit card debt only as a last resort.

These lines of credit aren't as readily available as they once were, but if you have equity in your home and a means to repay the debt, getting a home equity line can be good strategy.

4. Borrow against savings

If you have a 401(k) retirement plan through your employer, you can borrow up to $50,000 of your own funds. Be aware, however, that if you don't repay the full amount before you leave your job, whatever you still owe will be treated as a premature withdrawal subject to income tax penalties.

If you have an individual retirement account, or IRA, you can take out cash without incurring an income tax penalty as long as you prove you can repay the full amount within 60 days. Ensure you can pay the loan back within the allotted time or you can end up with bigger problems later.

5. Cut your spending

My experience has been that when people see their spending in black and white, they change their behavior. The first line of defense against a

---

personal cash crisis is to slash your budget so you're living within your current means

6. Pay off debt

One of the most rewarding times in my quest to become financially independent is when I paid off the car I currently own. The additional $735 per month is now being used to fund a retirement account. Many people have a mindset that they have to keep $5,000 in their bank account, but then they owe $1,000 on a credit card. They are paying 8 percent on the credit card and getting only 2 or 3 percent on the bank account. As with a home equity line, if you're paying 6 percent on a home equity line and yielding 2 percent or less on your checking account, you are losing every month.

Remember, that wealth is built one brick at a time not overnight. Developing good financial habits as written in this chapter will lead you to a place of financial stability and put you in position to never chase a paycheck again.

Now, you are ready for the next step to *Never Chasing A Paycheck Again*, creating income in Chapter 4!

Chapter Financial Principles

1. Financial success is never an accident.

2. To become financially stable, your habits must be intentional, deliberate and calculated.

3. You're never too broke to save money.

4. To begin to make the important transition from a paycheck-seeking life to a purpose-seeking life, it is important we develop good financial habits so that you save enough money to retire strong and leave a lasting legacy for your family.

5. If you find yourself saying, "I need a (whatever)," stop a moment and consider whether you really do.

6. If you can't pay your bill in full, stop using credit and perform plastic surgery on every personal credit card you have—cut them up today.

7. A couple of hundred dollars can make a difference. Always ensure you have at least $500 in the bank for emergencies and cushion by saving every cent you can.

8. The first line of defense against a personal cash crisis is to slash your budget so you're living within your current means.

Life Changing Answers Available in This Chapter

1. What can I do to generate my own income?

2. How can I earn more and work less?

3. How can passive income change my life?

4. How can I develop my idea into a commercial success?

Chapter 4

CREATE YOUR OWN INCOME

Creating your own income should be one of your primary goals in life.

While attending a financial seminar, the speaker said, "I've got good news and bad news."

"First, the good news: If you're anything like the average American earning at least $25,000 a year you will earn over a million dollars in your lifetime. Now, the bad news: If you're like most people, you'll spend nearly all of that money and retire with next to nothing." Unfortunately, the news is true for many of us.

Creating our own income and building wealth should be a goal of every human being. So how do you build wealth if you don't have any income-producing assets? And, what if like me you don't like to work hard for money? What should we be doing to build wealth?

For me, I was my only asset. By that I mean, if I didn't get out of bed and go to work somewhere then I didn't make any money that day. Other than me going to work every day, I didn't have any other income producing assets. The problem with this is if my "only asset" got sick or broke down, my ability to build wealth would have become limited. Without my daily involvement, my income potential would have disappeared.

I realized that I liked passive income much better than personally working for the money. Passive income is revenue that does not require your direct involvement. Some kinds of passive income you may be familiar with include owning rental property, royalties on an invention or creative work, and network marketing. (I am not involved in any network marketing companies although I believe in the concept.)

> Everyone needs to create and develop residual income.

The master key to earning more, working less and retiring early is to create income streams that do not require your direct involvement. The sooner you shift your focus on creating passive income, the sooner you can achieve personal and financial freedom.

To help you create your own income, let's first uncover two basic types of passive income, and a third type of income that, while technically not passive, is a key strategy for earning more and working less. Then, we'll create a model that best suits your financial and business needs.

Getting Paid Daily

Everyone needs to develop residual income. Residual income is revenue that occurs over time from work done one time. Some examples include:

- An author who creates a workbook and sells it in e-book format on the Internet

- A motivational speaker who produces a video that is sold in a bookstore

- An insurance agent who gets commission every year when a customer renews his policy

- A direct sales rep's income from her direct customers when they reorder product every month

- An aerobics instructor who produces a video and sells it at the gyms where she teaches

- A photographer who makes his photos available through a stock photography clearinghouse and gets paid a royalty whenever someone buys one of his images

As you can see, there are many different ways to generate residual income across a wide variety of opportunities. It may be recurring income from the same customers, or the sales of a product to new customers. Like an annuity that continues to pay monthly or yearly, many of these residual income-producing opportunities require your discipline to produce a product or create a service one time which could give you a life-time of financial benefits.

Notice that residual income is not merely *recurring* income. Recurring income may still require your involvement to earn the income, e.g., a writer on a weekly deadline, a consultant on a monthly retainer, or an executive coach with a bi-weekly appointment. This "active recurring income" offers some stability, but it also tends to an obligation. You still have limits on your earning capacity based on your own personal production capacity.

Leveraged Income

Leveraged income influences the work of other people to create income for you. Some examples of leveraged income include:

- A consultant outsources portions of his contract to another consultant

- An e-book author selling her e-book through affiliates who promote the product

- A general contractor who makes a profit margin on the work done by sub-contractors

- A network marketer who builds a down-line and receives commissions on the sales made by people in his down-line

- A restaurant owner franchises or sells her business model to other entrepreneurs

The key is that you are making money off of other people's labor and time, rather than primarily your own. Note that leveraged income may or may not also be residual income. When you combine the two strategies (residual and leverage), the income potential can be unlimited.

Skilled Leveraged Income

This is a term I use to describe income that requires your direct participation, but you can make more money with the involvement of more people. The key is to leverage your own personal skills which generally involve other people getting excited about your opportunity, such as:

- A seminar or training class that you teach
- A job opportunity that you create, such a janitorial business
- Networking events and other parties

Although these require your direct participation, your earning potential is much higher if you do them yourselves rather than paying someone else to do it for you. Here's a strategy that has worked for me. Fill a room with say, 100 people paying $24 each so that can cover your facility costs, marketing costs, and staffing fees. You will still have a nice chunk of change left over.

If you hire someone else to deliver the seminar or training, you will not make as much money, but you can devote your personal tasks on other opportunities; thus, increasing your income potential.

Here's how I benefited from the Skill Leveraged Income strategy. I have a large conference called "Conquer Worldwide". My first conference attracted over 2,500 aspiring entrepreneurs, professionals and business leaders. I charged $49 per person which covered all of my costs. I paid three speakers $5,000 each, paid for my facility costs and promotional fees and made a nice profit by leveraging my relationships and promotional skills.

You may have to start smaller, but start somewhere. Take a leap of faith!

Ideas to Create Your Own Income

You are surrounded by million dollar ideas every day; you just have to learn how to recognize them. Sometimes we don't recognize ideas because they are too close to us or they may require us to simply work the idea until it works for us.

Sometimes, all you need is a good idea to open new doors in your life. I invited several people to play golf with me some time ago. Afterwards, instead of talking about sports and other "guy stuff", I had an idea to talk to them about the importance of being a husband to their wives and being there emotionally for their children and being a good leader in their home.

Surprised by their responses, the discussion inspired the guys so much that we planned to do it the next month. When we met the next month, they didn't want to play golf, but wanted to meet and discuss men's issues, particularly as it related to character development, business and leadership. Six months later, more than 200 men were coming to the monthly meetings. I started a non-profit ministry called Kings & Priests. And to the fund the idea, I charged a membership fee of $325 a year. The group grew to thousands and it is sure to reach beyond a million members in the near future.

So how do you recognize a million dollar idea? I do believe that franchise "businesses-in-a-box" works for some aspiring entrepreneurs and direct sales organizations. Normally, they have a product and a training program that's ready to go. However, I am a firm believer that it is much more satisfying when you develop your own personal idea.

To find an opportunity that fits you perfectly, let's begin by triggering a business idea that you can use right now. Most successful businesses fall into one of the following categories. See if any of them trigger an idea for you:

- A spin-off from your present occupation
- A hobby or special interest
- An answer to the question, "Why isn't there a ...?"
- A shortcoming in others' products or services
- An observed need
- A technological advance
- A new way to use an ordinary thing.

Nothing comes to mind yet? As I wrote in Chapter 2, your true success is tied to your purpose and your God Given Talent. Let's find a few other clues about what you were born to do by answering the following questions:

- What problem in the world would you like to see solved?
- What do you do exceptionally well?
- If money was not an issue, what would you do for free to help people?
- What in the world gets you excited the most?
- What are you passionate about?
- What do you hate the most?
- What would you do to change the thing you hate?
- If you had to teach three subjects to students, what would they be?

What are your greatest assets? Let's take an inventory of what you currently have:

- ☐ The way you think
- ☐ Your confidence
- ☐ Your talents
- ☐ Your skills
- ☐ Your experience (including your past, good and bad)
- ☐ Your communication style
- ☐ Your attitude
- ☐ The way you look (contrary to popular opinion, there is no such thing as "ugly" only people who quit).

Everything in your life is worth something. Don't take anything in your life for granted. How many books have you read from people who had a horrific past who wrote a book and it turned into a hit made-for-TV movie? Perhaps the difference between them and you is they disciplined themselves to actually write the book. Someone else got excited about it and shared it with someone else. What if Oprah Winfrey got excited about your book? Your life would potentially change overnight.

When other people get excited about your life story, or past or any of your assets, they must pay for the right to use it. When that happens, your income increases!

Take My Reality Test

Now it's time to think about how to develop residual and leveraged income strategies in your life. Can you create an idea, a product or service that people will buy over and over again? Can you engage and motivate others to sell it? How could you make money off the work of others? The sooner you answer these questions, the sooner you'll have financial and personal freedom.

I have met many depressed "wannabe entrepreneurs" who have "tried" to launch new ventures but never really got the ideas off the ground. Or some people, like me many times in the past, have experienced some level of success only to crash and burn shortly after takeoff. And, worst yet, some people end up with "inventoritis". Inventoritis occurs when you have a garage full of products that you can't move or made an investment that won't pay off.

> Everything in your life is worth something and has value. Don't take anything in your life for granted.

So before you bet your life savings on your next million dollar idea, you should do a reality check to see if the idea is worth it. People often fall in love with their ideas and as a result can experience tremendous pain if it turns out the idea is a bad one.

Developing ideas into commercial successes is generally difficult work since there are many steps involved and the odds of success are not very high. You need to approach this with a process orientation and come at it with sufficient leadership skills and abilities to carry it though.

Trying to get rich on a one shot idea or expecting someone else to take the leadership initiative while you sit back and wait for a million dollar check to come in the mail will not work. It's going to take an attitude of dog-gone-it fortified with a persistence to pull it off repeatedly.

Famous American inventor Thomas Alva Edison was a master of developing ideas into commercial successes and died a rich and powerful man after a long prolific life. He produced over 1000 patented ideas, many of which were commercially successful.

Take my reality test. To help you perform a reality check on your idea, I have prepared a list of questions you can use as a way to determine whether or not you actually have an idea that is worth something. These questions will save you years of wasted time, money and heartache and help guide you to a brighter future. Anyone with an idea of launching a new business or considering an idea should take special note of the following reality test before launching out into the deep.

1. Do you know your 10 people who could potentially afford and purchase from you in the next 30 days?

2. Can you explain your idea to someone within 3 minutes or less?

3. Would media professionals be interested in your idea?

4. Can you define your marketing strategy in 5 words or less?

5. If someone stole your idea today, would you be willing to proceed anyway?

6. Are you willing to proceed if it costs twice as much and takes three times as long as your presumably reasonable estimates suggest?

7. Are you willing to take offer ownership in your company if required?

8. Do you have a network of credible and qualified advisors who will serve as your advisors?

9. If it fails, can you afford the losses?

10. Do you believe any of the following statements?

    - *"This idea will make millions."*
    - *"I have no competitors."*
    - *"I can do this on my own."*
    - *"Everyone will buy this."*
    - *"No one has thought of this."*
    - *"The marketing is no big deal."*
    - *"The product will sell itself."*
    - *"It's not about the money."*

If you believe any of the above statements about your idea, then your idea will cause *inventoritis* and you should stop right now until you are cured. These statements indicate idea failure and you will find yourself applying for a part-time job at Wal-mart. Get the condition treated first before proceeding.

If you idea passes my reality check, then conduct a brief research study. By this I mean invite several trusted friends or colleagues to your home or office and "pitch" your idea. Ask for honest feedback. If you have product, create samples to give away and ask for suggestions. Two things should happen. You may find a customer in your group and you will gain valuable intelligence about how you should price it.

If your idea fails my reality test, then move on knowing you haven't bet the bank, risked your job prematurely or unduly stressed your personal relationships. This is not the same thing as giving up on your ideas. It is much better to kill something that doesn't make sense than to have it kill you.

I've shared a lot of information, strategies and antidotes to help position you financially in the future. I look forward to hearing about your invention, product, service or idea. Your family and community will soon thank you.

Financial Principles
And My Personal Challenge to You

1. You are surrounded by million dollar ideas every day; you simply have to learn how to recognize them.

    What million dollar ideas have you thought about but haven't written down or put into action?

    _____

    _____

    _____

2. The master key to earning more, working less and retiring early is to create income streams that do not require your direct involvement.

    Do you agree? _____

3. The sooner you shift to focus on creating passive income, the sooner you can achieve personal and financial freedom.

    Are you prepared to change your focus to creating passive income? _____

4. Everyone needs to develop residual income.

    Take the time to consider how you can create residual income for yourself, family and others. Name four ways:

    1. _____

    2. _____

    3. _____

    4. _____

5. Creating your own your income and building wealth should be a goal of every human being.

   Is this a goal of yours? _____

   Have you written down your income and wealth-building goals for this year? _____

6. Leveraged income leverages the work of other people to create income for you.

   Write down the skill sets, education and talents of those closest to you. How can you leverage what they have to help you and them make money? _____

   _____

   _____

   _____

7. Sometimes we don't recognize ideas because they are too close to us and they may require us to work or be uncomfortable to develop them.

   Are you ready to work to develop your ideas? _____

8. Before you bet your savings on your next million dollar idea, you should do a reality check to see if the idea is worth it.

   Have you discussed your ideas with a trusted advisor? _____

9. Sometimes, all you need is a good idea to open new doors in your life.

What strategy do you have to help open the door for people to benefit from your idea?

_____

_____

_____

_____

10. Everything in your life is worth something.

What assets in your life have you taken for granted that other people value?

_____

_____

_____

_____

_____

<u>NOTES</u>

Life Changing Answers Available in This Chapter

1. With the job market in shambles, what is the best way to earn money in this new economy?

2. What life investment will give me the greatest return?

3. What should I do if things are not working in my life?

Chapter 5

SOLVE PROBLEMS AND GET PAID

Money is a reward for solving a problem in someone life.

It is interesting to watch my wife shop at the grocery store, especially as she shops down the aisle for cleaning products. I've seen her study labels on the back of each product searching for the best product that can solve a specific problem. Once she finds the cleaner that can undoubtedly solve the problem, she rewards the manufacturer with a sale. Money is simply a reward for solving a problem.

Likewise, you were created, purposed and gifted to solve a specific problem in someone's life. For example, mechanics solve car problems. Dentists solve teeth problems. Garbage men solve trash problems. Landscapers solve weed problems. Lawyers solve legal problems. When they solve their precise problem, they get paid. Every leader, entrepreneur, professional, business owner, father, mother and teacher wants to be known for solving precise problems in the lives of people. Solving problems give you power, influence and value.

As an ambitious person looking to improve your life, what specific problem have you been created to solve? Once you understand the precise problem you are to solve, your life will become more focused and you and your services will be in great demand.

Solving problems provide income, influence and financial provision for billions of people. The precise problem you have been gifted to solve may not have anything to do with your current vocation or education. This chapter will help you discover the precise problem you are to solve.

Helping You Find Opportunities

I've observed people who were chronically broke. Most of them are smart, intelligent and educated, however it was apparent to me they fell into one or more categories:

- They were unwilling to solve problems
- They were solving the wrong types of problems
- They were solving problems for the wrong people

A good friend gave me a great acronym for why some people are poor, meaning to be without adequate resources.

Consider the word *poor*: P.O.O.R.

Passed Over Opportunities Repeatedly!

An opportunity is any situation where your strengths, gifts or skills can be recognized and rewarded. How many opportunities do you pass over every day?

Every opportunity begins with a problem that someone needs to be solved. Another friend of mine, Glenn Henderson, was struggling financially several years ago. A friend of Glenn's needed to deliver 5 refrigerators from a location in Atlanta, Georgia, to some remote location in Africa. Glenn's friend didn't want to use FedEx or UPS because of the expense. Glenn saw an opportunity. Glenn got on the phone and called several local moving companies and commercial airliners that could pick up the refrigerators from Atlanta and deliver them to an airport in Africa.

Glenn then called several trucking companies in Africa to pick up the refrigerators from the African airport to make the final delivery. Glenn saved his friend thousands of dollars and made a few bucks himself. Glenn discovered that other people had similar delivery problems but didn't want the expense of using large corporations. Glenn launched his new company, AFC Express Worldwide. In 2007, AFC Express made more than $7 million as a new logistics company. Needless to say, he resolved his personal financial dilemma. It started with a problem and an opportunity.

> Every opportunity begins with a problem that someone needs solving.

If you discover that a company has slumping sales, they have a cash flow problem. Can you provide information, an idea or recommended strategy that can help solve the problem either temporarily or permanently? In my life as an entrepreneur, if my products, services, books and speaking engagements don't have the opportunity to solve problems today, it is guaranteed that I won't make any money today.

Whether it's engineering, customer service or janitorial, employers hire people for the purpose of solving a problem. Regardless of the job title, managers want to hire people who can solve a problem specifically for them. You were not hired by your company to generate more sales, or produce reports, or create products. They made a decision based on "who can best solve this particular problem." Once hired, the day you stop solving the specific problem you were hired to solve, is the day they seek to stop paying you.

In my sales seminars, I advise young sales people not to look for sales opportunities first, but rather ask the prospect about their problems (as it relative to your service). Once you convince the prospect you can solve the problem, the sale will be automatic and you have a friend for life.

Solving problems in the lives of others is the beginning of making additional income and starting a new life. Here are six money-making principles and questions for your consideration that can help you earn additional income right where you are.

<u>Money-making Principle #1</u>
The Types of Problem You Solve Determine
The Type of Income You Earn

Brain surgeons can make more than $5,000 an hour for their work while landscapers can make less than $10 an hour for their work. Both professions are needed almost on a daily basis somewhere in the country. Both professionals are worthy of compensation. To stay in business, both professions require expertise, focus and intellect. However, the type of problem that each professional *chose* to solve has uniquely different value.

What determines how much value people perceive you to have? The more unique the problem you solve, the greater the financial reward. If anyone can solve the problem or if the problem is already being solved by someone else, the less money people will pay.

My challenge to you:

- What consistent problem has your neighborhood, community or city had that you can help solve?

- What problems do your friends talk about that you can solve for a fee?

- What problems do your clients have outside of your job that you can fix?

Money-making Principle #2
Everyone has problems they are incapable of solving

The reason why roofers, bankers, psychologists, accountants, and bus drivers are necessary is because of a problem that needs a solution. Niche industries like marriage counselors were created simply because someone had a problem they couldn't solve.

My Challenge to You:

- Next time you meet with friends or associates, ask them, "What problem do you have that you are unable to solve?" You'll be surprised at their responses which could lead to your next career move. Whether their answers are personal, professional or business problem, take good notes. It is likely that many others in the same group have the same problems.

Money-making Principle #3
Your phone will never ring unless people have a problem they think you can solve.

Brain clutter makes marketing necessary. Clutter refers to the crowding and confusion in the marketplace caused by the unbelievable number of products people are trying to sell. There are too many competitors chasing too few dollars. Marketing is the skill of figuring out what people need then communicating that you can meet the need. You want to become known for solving one specific problem. You don't need a

SOLVE PROBLEMS AND GET PAID

million dollar budget, just a simple way to let people know who you are and what you do.

My Challenge To You:

1. Drive around your neighborhood and community and make a list of 40 problems you see. Include the simple problems such as overgrown grass to more complex problems such as homelessness.

2. Then, choose the top 10 problems that match your personal purpose (see Chapter 2).

3. Reduce the list to one problem.

4. Research the problem and possible solutions. Become an expert.

5. Then send an email, create a flyer, make a phone call or write a letter to people in the area that you have a solution to the problem.

6. Market the one problem and solutions.

Money-making Principle #4

The problem closest to you is the problem that could help you advance financially.

Ralph Waldo Emerson once said that "God hides things by putting them near us." The best opportunities are ideas hidden right under your nose.

My Challenge to You:

- What do you have in your house that can be a solution to someone's problem?

Money-making Principle #5
**The more skillful you are at solving problems
the more influence you will have.**

You'll either be known for the problems you create or the problems you solve. Politicians want to be known for solving community problems. Comedians want to be known for solving "sadness" problems. Mothers want to be known for solving emotional problems. And, the people who have excelled to the top of their industries did so because they solved the problems in their respective industries better than anyone else. No one wants to be known for creating problems.

My Challenge To You:

- What types of problems do you want to be known for solving?

- What problems are your competitors solving? How can you do it better?

Money-making Principle #6
**People will only seek you out for the
problems are you are known to solve.**

To best position yourself and your vision in the minds of people you must become known for solving one problem extraordinarily well. Since we live in the information age, people are faced with information overload; therefore people force everything into stereotypes then file it away in their minds. Everything is position according to reputation and advertising; people, products and places. There is not enough focus in people's minds to get the whole story. To stand out in the minds of people, you have to make people aware that you can solve a specific problem.

My Challenge To You:

- When people think of the value you bring to their world, what do they say?

- What do you do extraordinarily well to help people?

<u>Money-making Principle #7</u>
You are not created to solve everybody's problem.

As I wrote in Chapter 1 of this book, the only reason why smart people fail is because they lose focus. Again, focus on one specific problem and solve it extraordinarily well.

My Challenge To You:

- Are you charging a fee for solving a unique problem? If no, why not?

What To Do When Things Are Not Working

Imagine that you need money to launch a business but can't get a job or the money. One approach is to focus on the things that aren't working, and think about how you can fix them. This is the conventional approach to problem-solving. In many cases it's the right one to use. However plan cautiously, because all it does is bring you up to the same bland level as everyone else.

A better approach is to shift to a positive perspective, look at the things that *are* working, and build on them. In some situations this can be very powerful because, by focusing on positives, you can build the unique strengths which bring real success.

This is the premise behind "Appreciative Inquiry", a method of problem solving that was pioneered by David Cooperrider of Case Western Reserve University in the mid 1980s. To understand the basis of Appreciative Inquiry it is useful to look at the meaning of the two words in context.

- *Appreciation* means to recognize and value the contributions or attributes of things and people around us.

- *Inquiry* means to explore and discover, in the spirit of seeking to solve problems, and being open to new possibilities.

When combined, this means that by appreciating what is good and valuable in the present situation, we can discover ways to solve problems for a positive future.

Applying The "Appreciative Inquiry" To Your Situation

To apply Appreciative Inquiry to solve a situational problem, it's important to focus on positives. A positive approach helps you build on your strengths, just as conventional problem-solving can help you manage or eliminate your weaknesses.

The first step of the process is to identify and describe the problem you're trying to solve. From there you go on to look at the issue in five phases: **Define, Discovery, Dream, Design and Deliver**.

1. "Define" the Problem
Before you can analyze a situation, you need to define what it is you are looking at.

And, just as your decision to look at the positives will move you in a positive direction, defining your topic positively will help you look at its positive aspects. So, rather than seeking "Ways to Fix Lighting Problems At Your House", for example, you'll choose "Ways to Enhance Your Life at Home With Lighting or Ways to Enhance the Lighting in Your Home." This subtle change in wording can have huge implications for your focused solution.

2. "Discovery" Phase

Here you need to look for the best of what has happened in the past, and what is currently working well. Involve a sensible number of trusted people and design your questions to get people talking and telling stories about what they find is most valuable (or appreciated), and what has worked particularly well for you in the past.

When you've gathered enough raw information, analyze the data and identify the factors that most contributed to your past successes. What is most valued? What did people find most motivating or fun? What instills the greatest pride? And so on.

3. "Dream" Phase

In this phase, you can dream of "what might be" a solution. Think about how you can take the positives you identified in the Discovery phase, and reinforce them to build real strengths.

The way forward may be obvious from the results of the Discovery Phase. If it's not, a useful approach is to bring a diverse group of friends, associates and even former co-workers together and brainstorm creative ideas on what you could accomplish.

In our example, you might choose to enhance and build the good points that everyone likes about you, and use this as a strong message to attract potential clients, new relationships or resources during your problem solving process. You may also stop doing the things that aren't working, and use your time and money to reinforce the things that are.

Once you have agreed upon your dream or vision, you can take it to the Design phase.

4. "Design" Phase

Building on the Dream, this phase looks at the practicalities needed to solve the problem and support the vision. Here you start to drill down the types of systems, processes, and strategies that will enable the dream to be realized.

5. "Deliver" Phase

The last of the Ds is the implementation phase and it requires a great deal of planning and preparation. The key to successful delivery is ensuring that the Dream (vision) is the focal point. While the various parts of the team will typically have their own processes to complete, the overall result is a raft of changes that occur simultaneously throughout the organization, which serve to support and sustain the dream.

The "Deliver" phase of the cycle is not so much an end but a place to start to re-evaluate and continue the process of Appreciative Inquiry to continuously improve. Once you embrace the idea of positive change you can apply the cycle over and over again to various aspects of your life, and enjoy the positive outcomes that a positive perspective brings.

Chapter Principles
And My Personal Challenges to You

1. Money is a reward for solving a problem in someone's life.

   What problems does your co-workers, friends, neighbors or business owners in your city have that you could solve and charge a reasonable fee? List them here:

   a. _____
   b. _____
   c. _____
   d. _____
   e. _____
   f. _____

2. The problem you have been assigned to solve in your neighborhood, community, city or the world may not have anything to do with your current vocation or education.

   What natural gifts or talents do you have that have nothing to do with your education? List them:

   a. _____
   b. _____
   c. _____
   d. _____

3. Some people are chronically P.O.O.R. because they *Pass Over Opportunities Repeatedly.*

   What opportunities have you passed over that you can still take advantage of? _____

4. An opportunity is any situation where your strengths, gifts or skills can be recognized and rewarded.

   List the opportunities that your strengths, gifts and skills can benefit others financially.

   a. _____

   b. _____

   c. _____

   d. _____

   e. _____

   f. . _____

When launching your ideas, consider the following principles relative to the type of income you want to make:

5. The types of problems you solve determine the type of income you earn.

   What unique problem have you been created to solve?

   _____

   _____

6. Everyone has problems they are incapable of solving.

7. The greater the risk to solve someone's problem, the greater the reward.

8. Your phone will never ring unless people have a problem they think you can solve.

   List ways that you can let people know about the problem you can solve:

9. The problem closest to you is the problem that could help you advance financially.

10. The more skillful you are at solving problems the more influence you will have.

11. People will only seek you out for the problems you are known to solve.

   What do people seek from you now?

   _____

   What do you want to become known for? _____

   Are other people or companies charging a fee for what you are doing for free? _____

12. You are not created to solve everybody's problem.

NOTES

Life Changing Answers Available in This Chapter

1. How do make the transition from an employee to a full-time entrepreneur?

2. How will I know when it's time to quit my job to become an entrepreneur?

3. What are the practical steps to make the transition?

4. How do I get people to help me without paying them?

Chapter 6

FROM J.O.B. to OWNERSHIP

See a man diligent in his business, he shall stand before kings.
Proverbs 22:29

My father's success principle to me as a teenager was "Son, go to school, get a good job and stay there until you retire." He followed that principle by working on Ford Motor Company's assembly line for thirty-five years. I actually have the gold watch (not real gold, I might add) they presented to my father before he retired.

Ford Motor Company in Monroe, Michigan closed in 2009. Those jobs ceased to exist. The blue collar city of Monroe, Michigan, that I grew up in and loved is now depressed with high unemployment and oppressed with hopelessness.

What if my father's advise was go to school to learn how to develop my passion, launch my own business and build wealth for the next generation? What if he suggested producing a product or service and generating a profit which allowed me to hire others? What if he advised me to think like an entrepreneur rather than an employee? How different would my life be today? If those living in Monroe, Michigan were more entrepreneurial-mind rather than employee (paycheck-seeking)-minded?

Entrepreneurial-minded people make things happen in communities. Without these marketplace leaders, there would be no jobs, paychecks, office buildings, manufacturing plants, taxes or even malls and grocery stores. Entrepreneurial-minded people dream of better life, work hard to attract financial investment and take action. They are the risk-takers, the producers, the creators and the bosses.

Entrepreneurs, however, have the same financial challenges as everyone else. So this chapter is not about making money, but rather possessing the right mindset for long-term success. Having the right mindset will ultimately lead to increased income potential. Paychecks will ultimately follow you.

Minding Your Own Business
Entrepreneur- minded vs. Employee-minded
Which is better?

The debate regarding working in a corporate environment versus becoming an entrepreneur evokes many emotions. Many want to know "which is better?" and "why", and everyone has an opinion. It is not about you owning an actual business, but having an entrepreneurial mindset, and improving your quality of life.

The philosophical arguments are fun to listen to and evaluate, but get a "side hustle" to make ends meet, build wealth and leave a lasting legacy. A side hustle is when you work a job during the day but you work an additional business on the side at night.

When I was growing up in Monroe, everyone had a side hustle; some legal and some illegal. Some people gambled or did other illegal activities while others worked multiple jobs or joined network marketing plans. Typically one source of income was not enough to support our families and communities. The same holds true today. It's your individual choice about where and how you work, based on your individual circumstances, talents, skills, abilities, desires and fears.

Many of my pro-entrepreneur friends promote the glory of doing what they love, and having the freedom to make their own schedule. These are perfectly valid arguments.

> A side hustle is when you work a job during the day but you work an additional business on the side at night.

On the other hand, my pro-corporate supporters point out that access to important resources, education, and information is hugely facilitated by corporate environments. These are also perfectly valid arguments.

I'm a firm believer that each person decides upon a quality of life, and makes the proper decisions in order to support their preferences. True happiness does not exist just because you are an entrepreneur or a corporate employee. There are always tradeoffs in any situation and environment.

With more than twenty years of speaking at large conferences, coaching executives and working with people, here's what I've learned: People don't make changes unless they are unsatisfied with their current situation.

If you want to improve your situation, you must change your mindset. There are major differences between entrepreneur-minded people and employee-minded people. Let's examine these differences. If you are ready to make the transition, this chapter will help you get there.

Entrepreneur-minded People	Employee-minded People
Create jobs	Take jobs
Control their destiny	Have promotions, raises and professional destinies controlled by others
Have potential for very big payoff	Have consistent, but low payments
Owns the company	Can be fired at any time, mostly for any reason
Can get access to significant business credit	Harder to obtain significant credit
Willing to take educated risks	Mostly risk adverse
Value wealth as security	Value job security
Pay taxes only on NET income	Pay income tax on total income
Invest with inside knowledge	Invest with limited, outside knowledge
Seek business opportunities	Seek a better job
Have assets other than himself/herself to create wealth	In most cases, they are their only money-producing asset
Can become rich at young age	Will not become financially secure without years of hard work
Create the system	Must live by the system and the bureaucracies
Able to use all their skills	Only able to use limited skills
Hire whoever they want	Have very little say in who they work with
Working to build wealth so that 401(k) pension is not needed	Working to contribute to 401(k) pension plan
Rarely does the same thing everyday	Often has daily routine
Make money while they sleep	Only make money at work

Making The Transition

Over the past 20 years of dealing with people of all incomes in my speaking and business career, the number one question asked is "how do I make the transition from working for someone else to working for myself fulltime?" Let's examine this question in what I call *The 6 Irrefutable Laws of Transition.*

These laws are in no particular order. You must totally commit to obeying each law in your personal and professional life to get the results. They should be pursued and taught to everyone around you. In other words, make it a vital part of your personality and you will eventually see change. Here are the laws:

- Law 1:   Everything depends on your reputation; guard it with your life.

- Law 2:   Plan all the way to the end

- Law 3: Create products and services that solve ordinary problems.

- Law 4:   Treat everyone as if they could be your next customer

- Law 5:   Select a Life Board of Directors For Protection and Expansion Purposes

- Law 6:   Put ALL your trust in God, not man

<u>Law 1</u>

Everything depends upon your reputation –
Guard it with your life

An outstanding reputation is the cornerstone of respect, power and influence. Even God says in the Bible that a good reputation is better than money or expensive perfume (Ecclesiastes 7:1). Work hard to make your reputation unassailable.

Since it's virtually impossible to truly know and understand friends, associates, colleagues, strangers or prospects, we make assumptions relative to people's character based on appearances. We analyze what is visible to our eyes – clothes, gestures, actions, words, habits. While integrity and honesty are the necessary foundations of long term success, it takes time to see these qualities. So in the social realm, appearances are the barometer in which most people judge another person's character. One false slip could damage to a person's reputation affecting their career, business, ministry, finances and other aspects of life.

Your reputation is important because it is the one thing that people can point to that is of your own creation. Your reputation, good or bad, protects you in the game of appearances and gives you a degree over how the world judges you.

You may say, "Robert, I don't really care how people see me." In this case, you could gain a reputation of arrogance and insolence. By not caring how others perceive you, you let others decide for you. Successful people control their reputations and images by intentionally positioning themselves in the minds of people.

Reputation works like a credit report: it can draw resources and relationships to you and add to your wealth and influence or it can repel critical resources and relationships from you and weaken your power and influence in the world. It's all based on how you choose to live your life and how you treat people.

In the beginning, you should work to establish your reputation for one extraordinary quality, whether it is for doing the right thing, being the best in the industry, delivering your services on time, or honesty. This quality will set you apart and get others talking about you or your company. As your good reputation spreads, people and their resources will be naturally drawn to you. People and companies with stellar reputations don't have to look too far to find meaningful partnerships. It's those with less than stellar reputations that struggle.

A strong reputation amplifies your strengths and increases your presence without you spending a lot of energy. A solid reputation will also create an aura of respect and in some cases it cause "reverential fear". During World War II fighting in the North African desert during World War II, the German general Erwin Rommel had a reputation for deceptive maneuvers that struck fear in the hearts of their enemies. On one occasion, General Rommel's tanks were outnumbered five to one, however, an entire British city evacuated upon the news that General Rommel was approaching. A strong reputation will financially benefit you even when you are not in the room.

> A solid and strong reputation can produce opportunities for you, event when you are not in the room. Guard it with your life.

As I heard, your reputation precedes you, and if it garners respect, a lot of your work is done for you.

Perhaps you have stained your reputation through a bad business deal or a previous poor decision and it has been difficult to establish a new one. Consider partnering with someone with a reputation that exceeds your own. Get permission to use their image or good name. It is complicated to erase a reputation of dishonesty and deceit but many politicians, celebrities, professionals, relatives and friends have overcome this challenge. They have made comebacks by coming clean with those around them and convincing them of their turnaround.

<u>Law 2</u>
Plan all the way to the end

The ending is everything. Plan your transition through to the end, taking into account all the possibilities good and bad, understanding challenges and setbacks. By planning to the end, you will be prepared for surprises and avoid being overwhelmed by negative circumstances that will arise.

If detailed planning is so important, why do most people avoid it? Most people are too imprisoned by day-to-day life to plan with foresight and vision. It is difficult for them to ignore immediate worries and pleasure to properly plan the rest of the lives. You have the power to set back from your circumstances and overcome the natural tendency to react as things happen as opposed to initiate possibilities to make them as they should be.

> Many people have tried to succeed without a written plan...it rarely works out as expected.

If you ask most people about their future, most will say they are aware of their future and know what's ahead. However, upon further inquiry, they will tell me only what they want to happen, in accordance with their desires, not a written script.

Most people have vague plans based on their imaginations, not reality, research or investigation. Typical vague planning focuses on a happy ending with fortune, wealth and pleasures concluding their vague dream.

Your planning must be crystal clear and it must remain in the forefront of your mind and visible daily at home. The best way to avoid crisis is to anticipate them. Distractions, jealous people and the world will try to knock you off track. Anything you do that is rewarded with financial success takes hard work. You know difficulties are coming, this time prepare for it with written solutions, answers and reversals.

Law 3
Create products and services that
can solve every day problems

Every person, family and organization have problems they can't solve without help from a product or service. And, the people and companies who can solve specific problems in easy and convenient ways succeed and grow much faster than those that don't.

Look for people and organizations in trouble and create ways to solve their problem. For example, my friend, Glenn Henderson, had a contact that needed to deliver 10 refrigerators from a city in United States to a city in South Africa. Glenn called several airlines, trucking and delivery companies both in the United States and in South Africa. Through research and a couple of hours spent on the telephone, Glenn was able to deliver his contact's refrigerators to their destination within two and half days. From there, Glenn started a company called AFC Worldwide Express, a global transportation and logistics company. His company grossed over $2 million in 2008. It all started with creating a service that solved a problem.

Law 4
Treat everyone as if they could be your next client

You are always one relationship away from your next big contract or a key financial miracle.

Remain sensitive to your surroundings because your next introduction could change your life. Six degrees of Separation (also referred to as the "Human Web") refers to each person who is known by one of the people they know, and then everyone is at most six steps away from any other person on Earth. Facebook, currently one of the leading social networking sites on the internet, created a platform application named "Six Degrees" developed by Karl Bunyan. He calculated the degrees of separation between different people. It has about 4.5 million users (as of April 2009), as seen from the group's page. The average separation for all users of the application is 5.73 degrees, whereas the maximum degree of separation is 12.

Your most valuable assets are honesty and generosity. Use them every day with everyone you meet.

<u>Law 5</u>
Select a Life Board of Directors For
Protection and Expansion Purposes

Everyone needs accountability. And, the more successful you become, the more accountability you need.

One of the greatest assets in my life is what I call my Life Board of Directors. I first learned this concept when I read the book *Dare To Succeed* by Van Crouch. A Life Board of Directors cares about you, your business, your family, your relationship with God. I have lunch with my Life Board at least once a quarter. I submit my plans and goals to them and help me stay on track.

My LBs (as I refer to them) asks me critical questions such as how's your relationship with your wife. How's your relationship with your daughters? Are you still planning to sign the office lease? Can you really afford it? How's your relationship with God? Do you still pray and attend church regularly?

I've learned that you are nobody until somebody expects something of you. If you want to do anything significant with your life, you must be willing to be held accountable. A group of caring, smart people can provide you with sound counsel and support when you need it. To make the transition, surround yourself with people who care enough to hold you accountable.

Law 6
Put ALL your trust in God, not man

Launching a new business or transferring from being an employee to an entrepreneur will be one of the hardest things you will ever do. You need God's help, direction and guidance to get you through the tough nights or when all your planning has failed. Your faith, belief and hope needs to be in God's word, not in your limited abilities, banks or people.

Your vision is bigger than you. That's way the Bible says, "Some trust in their war chariots and others in their horses, but we trust in the power of the Lord our God" (Psalms 20:7). In other words, as the leader of your vision, your trust should not be in your money, your skill, your possession or your wealth, but in God and His ability to help you get things done on a daily basis.

Make The Leap

Making the leap from working for someone to working for yourself begins with the way you think. You must believe that you were created to conquer the world but yet be gentle enough to understand the needs of ordinary people. You must believe that your product or service can change people's lives.

And, yes, you are the one that God chose to deliver the solution to your client's problem. Entrepreneurship is a calling. Obey the call, keep moving and don't look back.

NOTES

Chapter Financial Principles
And My Personal Challenges to You

1. People don't make changes unless they are unsatisfied with the current situation.

    What are ways you can change the things you are unsatisfied with in your life?

    _____

    _____

    _____

2. An outstanding reputation is the cornerstone of respect, power and influence.

    What one thing do you want to be known for?

    _____

3. In this economy, everyone needs a "side hustle".

    Do you have one? _____

Use the following principle to help you make the transition from employee to entrepreneur.

4. People and companies who can solve specific problems in easy and convenient ways succeed and grow much faster than those that don't.

5. Plan your transition through to the end, taking into account all the possible twists, setbacks, consequences or misfortunes that could reverse your hard work.

6. When starting out, you will have to do the majority of the tasks yourself.

7. Remain sensitive to your surroundings because your next introduction could change your life.

8. Everyone needs accountability. And, the more successful you become, the more accountability you need.

9. Launching a new business or transferring from being an employee to an entrepreneur will be one of the hardest tasks you will ever do. You will need God's help.

10. Your vision is bigger than you, always staff to your weakness.

NOTES

Life Changing Answers Available in This Chapter

1. How can my confidence help me win contracts and opportunities?

2. If I lost my confidence, how can I rebuild it?

3. If I have low self-confidence, what can I do to become confident?

Chapter 7

CONFIDENCE MAKES THE DIFFERENCE

Do not throw away your confidence, for it carries a great and glorious compensation of reward. ~ *Hebrews 10:35*

My first opportunity to fund a major real estate deal was a disaster. I nearly lost everything.

I had the meeting of a life time with a private equity firm who built their business financing commercial real estate projects. They verbally approved the deal, researched my background and were excited about my deal. This deal would solve all of my financial issues, pay off my house, put my daughter through college and put my family on financial Easy Street. So I thought.

Once I got into the meeting and began to pitch my project, I was nervous, fumbling and overly apologetic. While the project was right up their ally and the written presentation was great, they basically smiled, shook my hand and showed me the door. I found out later they had confidence in the project but did not want to take a risk on someone who was not confident in their abilities to deliver. Self-confidence was the missing ingredient and I lost a million dollar deal.

Likewise, we rely on the quiet confidence of our doctors to present their diagnosis; we enjoy the star-quality confidence of an inspirational speaker and the steadfast confidence of an entertainer to hold a room. Self-confident people exude qualities that everyone admires.

People who lack self-confidence experience difficulty succeeding at anything. Normally, people without self-confidence are usually employees following people with high self-confidence.

Self-confident people inspire confidence in others, their peers, bosses, audiences, customers, and friends. Gaining the confidence of others is one of the key ways in which a self-confident person finds success.

> People who lack confidence find it difficult to succeed at anything. However, when practiced, confidence can be learned, maximized and developed.

The **good news** is that self-confidence really can be learned, developed and maximized. And, whether you're working on your own self-confidence or building the confidence of people around you, it's well-worth the effort! All other things being equal, self-confidence is often the single ingredient that distinguishes a successful person from someone less successful.

During the blistering hot summer of 1983, I found myself in basic training serving in the U.S. Army's infamous Tank Hill in Ft. Jackson, South Carolina. In addition to the scorching sun, the annoying bugs, the heavy back packs and the endless days without adequate sleep, we meet Drill Sergeant Jackson. When drill sergeant Jackson stepped on the platform to gather the troops for the morning roll call at 5 a.m., I remember him doing it with inspiring confidence. Even at 5 a.m., his boots were shined, his voice commanded attention and his presence communicated that he was in charge.

I was a young man at the time, but I remember being inspired for the first time by Sergeant Jackson's confidence to move the entire company of almost 200 soldiers in one direction and in unison. I had never dreamt of possessing such confidence to move other people, but I knew in order to succeed it was important. I relied on his confidence to get through two tough months of basic training.

I am still inspired by Sergeant Jackson's confidence today and have used it to inspire others around the world through my books, live events, CDs, teaching materials, media interviews, television shows and other events.

Your self-confidence is key to never chasing a paycheck again.

What's Your Confidence Score?

Your level of self-confidence shows in many ways: Your behavior, body language, speech, and so on. Look at the comparisons below and take the following test to judge your confidence level. Score yourself on both "Low self-confidence" and "High self-confidence" with zero being the lowest and 10 being the highest.

Low Self-Confidence 0 to 10	High Self-Confidence 0 to 10
My actions and behavior is typically based on what other people think. *Score* _____.	My daily actions and behavior based on what I believe to be right, even as others criticize me for it. *Score* _____.
You typically stay in your comfort zone to avoid taking risks or offending others. *Score* _____.	You have taken calculated risks in the past and went the extra mile to achieve better results. *Score* _____.

You routinely talk down to yourself when you make a mistake. *Score* _____ .	You have learned how to turn nervous energy into positive energy typically with good results. *Score* _____ .
You prefer to cover mistakes before anyone can find out. *Score* _____ .	You have no problem admitting a mistake while vowing to learn from them. *Score* _____ .
You find it difficult at times to speak up in meetings when you have something important to say. *Score* _____ .	You are known for communicating and introducing new ideas. *Score* _____ .
At times, you can act "shy" around strangers. *Score* _____ .	In meetings, you look people in the eye, firmly shake their hand and speak with authority. *Score* _____ .

Total Low Self-Confidence
Score _____

Total High Self-Confidence
Score _____

Now total each column and compare the two scores; which score is higher? If your low self-confidence score is higher than your high self-confidence score, then you have to work to do. If your high self-confidence score is higher than your low confidence score but less than 50, then you need improvement in this area. A score of 10 or more in Low Self-Confidence area can be self-destructive to your future and sabotage your success.

However, regardless of your race, creed, religion, gender or background, a score of 60 in the High Self-Confidence column is achievable.

As we will read later in this chapter, low self-confidence can be self-destructive, and it often seen and communicated as negativity. Self-confident people are generally more positive – they believe in themselves and their abilities, and they also believe in the wonders of living life to the fullest.

Get Rid of Low Confidence

So how do you build this sense of balanced self-confidence, founded on a firm appreciation of reality? There is no quick fix, or 3-miniute antidote or magical pill. Here are four reasons why most people have low-confidence.

1. **Loss of Confidence.** Some people with low-confidence had a healthy dose of confidence at some point in their life but a bad experience or series of setbacks destroyed it. In this case, their confidence simply needs to be restored. Like a professional baseball player whose batting average has gone down; his technique is good but his confidence is lost. A good coach will understand the psychology of the player and restore his confidence above his technique.

2. **Insecurity.** Other people with low-confidence are simply not secure or comfortable with the way God made them. They feel inadequate or without support so they shrink into an insecure personality or worst yet, they take on someone else's persona.

3. **Unpreparedness.** There is never an excuse for not being prepared. Unpreparedness almost always causes others to lose confidence in you and will contribute to your low self-confidence.

4. **Self-doubt.** Uncontrolled negative inner self-talk will talk you in low-confidence. It will come out in your attitude, behavior, facial expressions and dress.

The good news is that building self-confidence is readily achievable, just as long as you have the focus and determination to carry things through. And what's even better is that the things you'll do will build success – after all, your confidence will come from real, solid achievement. No-one can take this away from you!

Building high self-confidence has two requirements: Inner requirement and outer requirements. By using these *10 strategies*, this will give you the mental edge you need to surpass your potential.

Inner Requirements:

1.   Control your inner chatter

How you talk to yourself matters.   If you are allowing yourself to say things like, "I can't afford the life I want", or "I'm gonna always be broke", or "I'm a colossal failure". The way you talk to yourself internally is seen by others externally through your attitude, clothing, appearance,   posture and etc. Your inner conversation affects your confidence negatively or positively, depending upon what you hear. You can only fake it for so long until the real you comes out either through pressure or a circumstance. So it's best to control your thought life by meditating on affirmations and bible scriptures. Talk to yourself out loud and tell yourself, "I will be successful", "Things will get better", "I will be wealthy". My point is when you open your mouth; your mind has to stop to listen. By doing this you are actually telling your mind what to think.

2.   Be Comfortable With You and Your Body

Wealthy and successful people come in all sizes, shapes and colors. So it doesn't matter how big, small, thin, dark, or pale you are. What's important to confidence is how you view yourself. With an improper view of yourself and your body size or shape, you will become tentative, shy and inhibited. Being comfortable in your own skin is a journey. Here are a few ways you get comfortable with yourself and your body.

- Never compare your or body type to anyone else's.
- Accept your flaws. Make fun of them when appropriate. It will make you be comfortable with your imperfections and other people will laugh with you, not at you.
- Set your mind to exercise for health purposes rather than for cosmetic purposes
- Remind yourself of how great you are and wonderful God made you.

3.   Know What You Are Talking About

I subscribe to the philosophies that if you don't know what you are talking about, then just say nothing. I have lost contracts and contacts simply by opening my mouth and sounding ignorant of the subject at hand. This normally occurs when you are trying to impress people. Never seek to impress anyone with your knowledge but seek to engage others through asking questions and then listen. This builds confidence. For example, a supervisor who listens well will tend to have better self-esteem and self-image because they will get along better with others.

4.   Understand that God is with you always

I enjoy what Hebrew 10:35 says about confidence:

> *Do not throw away your confidence,*
> *for it carries a great and glorious compensation of reward.*

Essentially, the Bible is instructing us to keep our confidence in God for it will one day reward us. I don't believe the compensation will be only given in the Heaven but here on earth. While I am talking about the importance of self-confidence in this chapter, however, the beginning of our self-confidence comes from our belief that God is with us always. He will not allow us to fall, fail or decrease.

Outer Requirements:

5.   Speak Up

I read a report stating that most people would rather die than speak in front of a group of people. I submit that the majority of these fearful respondents simply lack confidence. In small group discussions, many people never speak up because they're afraid that people will judge them for saying something stupid. This fear isn't really justified. Generally, people are much more accepting than we imagine. In fact most people are dealing with the exact same fears. By making an effort to speak up at least once in every group discussion, you'll become a better public speaker, more confident in your own thoughts, and recognized as a leader by your peers.

6.   Work Out

Along the same lines as personal appearance, physical fitness has a huge effect on self confidence. If you're out of shape, you'll feel insecure, unattractive, and less energetic. By working out, you improve your physical appearance, energize yourself, and accomplish something positive. Having the discipline to work out not only makes you feel better, it creates positive momentum that you can build on the rest of the day.

7.   Walk with Purpose

The new term that teenagers have coined for confidence is "swagger", which is defined as to walk or conduct oneself with an insolent or arrogant air; strut. Basically, they are referring to a "star quality" type of confident walk. The obvious danger is that swagger can turn people off. Swagger is fine if done with a purpose. Walking faster while acknowledging people along your walk will cause your confidence to be seen. However, walking fast and ignoring people will certainly be seen as arrogance.

8.   Posture

Nothing says "low confidence" like a sagging, slouching posture. When you have your back arched and your head stuck out and down, it shows a lack of confidence. No one wants to follow a person with that type of posture. A tango instructor said it well: Stand as if you own the world. I learned this from one of my coaching clients who was taking dance lessons. Don't overdo it, but think highly of yourself (you will stand taller), and the world will notice and react accordingly.

Great posture adds to your stature and presence. When you walk into the room, your strong posture should turn heads. Here's how you strengthen your posture: Envision the John Hancock Building in Chicago, one of the tallest in the world. Now, stand up. Imagine your body is a tall, narrow building and plant your feet 8-10 inches apart. Now, make sure your knees are directly above your heels, hips above your knees, stomach above your hips, chest above your stomach and head above your chest - such that if you took a piece of heavy string and dropped it from your nose, it would fall between your feet. Keep this image in mind as you stand around at networking events, meetings and receptions.

9. Dress above your environment

Have you noticed that your self confidence levels differ according to the clothes you wear? Have you noticed that when you wear a certain suit or shirt you tend to become more self confident?

Your Self Confidence is strongly related to your self image, which is the mental image you have for yourself in your mind. Fortunately, your subconscious mind does not differentiate between your body parts and the clothes you wear and so it considers clothes an extension to your body. The result is that your self image differs according to the clothes you wear and so does your self confidence. Want to know how to make use of this? Relative to confidence, it's not necessarily "what" you wear but "how" you wear what you have on. Ensure your dress shoes are highly shined; finger nails cleaned, pants or dress pressed. These minor details communicate confidence and that you care about your job.

If you overdress (which is rare but can happen) or under dress (the more likely scenario), the people who you are trying to lead may feel that you don't care enough about the job. Dressing conservatively is always the best policy. The latest fashion may not always be suiting you or the occasion; it could be damaging. The bottom line is, choose your clothes wisely clothing contributes to your confidence.

10. Over The Top Self-Confidence

Self-confidence is about balance. At one extreme, we have people with low self-confidence. At the other end, we have people who may be over-confident.

If you are under-confident, you'll avoid taking risks and stretching yourself; and you might not try at all. And if you're over-confident, you may take on too much risk, stretch yourself beyond your capabilities, and crash badly. You may also find that you're so optimistic that you don't try hard enough to truly succeed.

Getting this right is a matter of having the right amount of confidence, founded in reality and on your true ability. With the right amount of self-confidence, you will take informed risks, stretch yourself (but not beyond your abilities) and work hard.

Chapter Principles
And My Personal Challenges to You

1. Never seek to impress anyone with your knowledge but seek to engage others through asking questions and then listen. This builds confidence.

    List several questions here that you can use to engage influencers at your next networking event:

    a. _____

    b. _____

    c. _____

    d. _____

- People who lack self-confidence, however, find it difficult to succeed at anything.

    Do you agree? _____

- Self-confident people exude qualities that everyone admires.

    List the qualities (positively or negatively) you believe you exude.

    a. _____

    b. _____

    c. _____

    d. _____

Would the people who are closest to you agree with your above list? How can you change the negative qualities (if any) into a positive?

- The good news is that self-confidence really can be learned, developed and maximized.

- All other things being equal, self-confidence is often the single ingredient that distinguishes a successful person from someone less successful.

- Self-confident people are generally more positive – they believe in themselves and their abilities, and they also believe in the wonders of living life to the full.

- Being comfortable in your own skin is a journey.

- People with low-confidence are simply not secure or comfortable with the way God made them.

- Accept your flaws. Make fun of them when appropriate. It will make you comfortable with your imperfections and other people will laugh with you, not at you.

- Nothing says "low confidence" like a sagging, slouching posture.

Life Changing Questions Answered
In This Chapter

1. What is the master key to making money on the Internet

2. What are 6 ways I can start making additional income, now?

3. What tools do I need to produce income, now?

Chapter 8

MAKE YOUR MONEY WORK FOR YOU

"...but money answers all things." ~ Ecclesiastes 10:19

An estimated 1.3 billion people use the internet everyday for business and personal purposes. Others "go online" for relationship development and communication reasons. However, according to the U.S. Census Bureau, total e-commerce sales for 2008 were $133.7 billion and that number is expected to exceed to $250 billion by 2015. With internet advertisers spending more than $34 billion annually, doesn't it make sense to make a portion of your new income on the internet?

I've had several well-paying jobs in my short life with all of the benefits and joys of working from home. But I was never happy or fulfilled because I still had to work in many cases 50 to 70 hours a week to make ends meet. I was constantly tired with no hope of getting off the corporate treadmill.

Instead of chasing a paycheck, I needed to find other ways to bring money into the house so that I could pursue my life's calling. I tried just about everything to make money but rarely did anything ever work out the way I had planned. When you are trying to change your life, you'll try just about anything.

I discovered making money on the internet can be fun and easy with the same benefits, if you know what you are doing. A large portion of my businesses come from memberships, book sales, online coaching and other services.

In this chapter, you will find many proven income-producing ideas to help you uncover opportunities and provide what I call "income insight". Income insight is where you see an opportunity to make money that other people cannot see.

How To Make Money On-line

Some people have dreamed about owning their own business and have not followed through because of the investment in resources. However, the Internet allows people to at least try without making a large initial investment.

Mark Zukerberg had a dream of owning his own Internet business and created a social networking website called Facebook. Several years later, Microsoft, the computer giant, valued Facebook at $15 billion and invested $240 million for a 1.6% stake in Mark's company. You can envy Mark's success or become a part of the revolution on the web.

> You can envy other people's internet success or become a part of the revolution.

Internet profit opportunities vary dependent upon your business model. You can make money from advertising, subscriptions or straight sales. If you are thinking about launching an online business, it may require only a few hundred dollars in equipment, while others demand significant hardware and perhaps even a warehouse. And all involve various levels of time, capital and technological skill.

Craigslist is another start up that is now worth a reported $3 billion with 25 or more employees. It charges businesses to post help wanted ads in various major cities and now collects subscription fees for its members. More than 5 billion people visit Craigslist every month.

Monetizing one's website can be a difficult task. To attract large advertisers to your site, you will need to have at least 500,000 unique visitors per month. Advertisers are mainly interested in "click throughs" which tends to be below one-half of 1 percent. Even large advertisers can be reluctant to pay big money to advertise on large sites.

> The key to making money on the Internet is **connectivity.** By this I mean, by connecting the unconnected to the connection, you create value.

Subscription-based models can be even more difficult, but not impossible, to monetize. Unless your site fulfills an immediate need (i.e. a potential mate, a loan for a mortgage, a downloadable business document, etc.), visitors aren't likely to pay for the content.

One way to garner subscription revenue is to run a virtual marketplace. These sites make money by allowing buyers and sellers easy access to each other. Dating sites like eHarmony.com and Match.com charge a subscription fee to access their members. Another example is Mfg.com which matches equipment manufacturers with smaller component suppliers. And H2Bid.com links municipalities with wastewater-equipment vendors.

As the Internet grows, so will the sophistication of the business models. Take 4 year old 23andme.com. They offer something that has never been sold before to the masses, your DNA (literally). They sell it for medical reasons for those that are predisposed to prostate cancer, glaucoma, heart disease and other life-threatening illnesses. In 2009, it will also provide social networking between customers who share traits ranging from ethnic origins to disease profiles. This type of model brings together solutions and people around a unique cause amongst members.

The Master Key To Making Money on the Internet

I am not suggesting that you spend your time building an internet company, but use the net as a tool to create value and get paid. Use the internet as a tool, not as an end; whether you are part of a big organization or a sole business owner

Since we are living in the information age, the internet has become the primary source of information for 80% of all adults. You can have a free website built in about 10 minutes regardless of your skill level and now there are professional website builders that will actually allow you to build your website like on weebly.com. With a little more effort, you can even add pictures and videos to your website. People buy all kinds of stuff over the internet, from furniture to pets to automobile parts. You can even have your own online yard sale.

So how do you make money on the internet? From all of my examples above we can determine the key to making money on the Internet is **connectivity.** By this I mean, by connecting the unconnected to the connection (i.e. seller, information, opportunity etc.), you create value.

- Connect people buying with people who are selling.
- Connect people who are proximate geographically.
- Connect advertisers to people who want to be advertised to.
- Connect job hunters with jobs.
- Connect information seekers with information.
- Connect teams to each other.

- Connect those seeking similar information.
- Connect partners and those that can leverage your work.
- Connect organizations spending money with ways to save money.
- Connect like-minded people into a movement.

Regardless of the product or service, the common denominator of most top money-grossing websites is connecting people exceptionally well. Find a reason to connect people and build your website around it.

6 More Ways To Make Even More Money

We've devoted a lot of time discussing income potential opportunities and ideas for you to ponder. I hope something clicked in your mind and heart that you can immediately launch. Here are 6 additional ways to make even more money.

Become an Info-preneur

The most exciting opportunity in this new millennium is *information marketing*. An entrepreneur whose main product is information is called an infopreneur. You can have enough information and experience in your head right now that can produce a life-time of income. For example, everyone has at least one book or article that can be written and published and turned into modest income. Self-publish the work yourself and sell it at a profit. Start with writing your personal story; it doesn't require any time-consuming research and it can be written based on your experience and passion. Your story could land you on a television talk show or become a movie. You could travel on the speaking circuit lecturing on topics that interest you and help others. These opportunities can start with information that you already have in your possession.

Sell Your Expertise

There are companies that allow people to give advice on their topic of expertise by video-chatting. Here's how it works: You as an advisor receives calls from clients that is previously set for you. Advisors set their rate and can decide when to start charging a client during a session. Clients pay directly through PayPal and may also schedule an appointment in advance. In many cases, the company will provide with a telephone line in your home or office. Some people make as much as $5,000 a month. Research the companies that offer you the best rates.

Use Classified Ads – Simple But Powerful

Classifieds are a powerful, inexpensive method of reaching new customers. A short, well-written classified ad leading prospects to visit your website or phone number can do wonders for your business. I've actually done this and made lots of money. I contacted a manufacturer of children's video tapes and asked them if I could wholesale their merchandise. They were happy to oblige. Every company is looking for hundred percent commissioned-based sales people. After I worked out a price per video deal with the manufacturer and a separate deal for them to drop ship the product, I then called several newspapers and bought several inexpensive classified ads. I wrote ads advertising *"Classic low-priced children's videos produced by world-class producers delivered to your home in two days, call me at 404..... for more information."* I marked up the video by one hundred percent to equal the price of similar children's videos found in local stores. That one ad placed in about 20 newspapers produced enough money for me to purchase a used car.

Become a Power Solution-Seller

The master key to a successful sales strategy is to define your customers and zero in on their needs with a focused solution. Write a short, targeted sales letter to highly-focused target markets of prospects.

Your correspondence should focus on their individual problem that your product or services solves. People pay for solutions to their problems.

Ask, "What Can I Do For You?"

Continually ask the question, "What else can I do for you." If you ask it, you may be pleasantly surprise with the responses. It will cause people to pause and actually think about your question. Their response could lead to additional business. A large chain increased sales by a billion dollars by asking their customers if they would like to "super size their meal" after every order. You can use this strategy in your everyday conversation to help launch new services.

Become an On-line Power Broker

You can sell your hottest and latest products and even old items laying around your house on websites like eBay or uBid. This can be an easy way to generate immediate income and attract new customers. Ebay and uBid makes it extremely affordable to set up your on-line business. Simply following a few simple instructions can help you to mine the gold that already exists in your house. From golf clubs, shoes, old television sets, furniture to picture frames, tools and lawnmowers, if it can be shipped, it can probably be offered and sold on eBay or uBid. You'll be surprised at how many people are interested in your stuff.

Army veteran Brandi Ramos of Springfield, Ill., did it. As a single mom in need of extra income, she started her online retail career peddling "big and tall" men's clothing on eBay.

Three years later, Ramos, 32, makes a good living working online out of her 600-square-foot basement packed with hanging displays and baker's racks piled with tupperware containing underwear and belts. She claims to net $25,000 on $100,000 sales a year, and even earns a few bucks per order on shipping.

Use e-Newsletters

One of the easiest ways to build your brand and gain wide exposure for your small business is to produce an e-Newsletter. An eNewsletter will help you keep in touch with your target market and offer them insights and tips to help them build their business. The greatest benefit is that an E-newsletter will position you as an expert and will build your brand perhaps globally. At the end of your tip or article, offer a product or service that supports the article and an electronic way for the prospect to purchase it (Paypal.com or a merchant service that accepts credit cards).

Chapter Principles
And My Personal Challenges to You

1. The Internet allows people to at least try to own their own business without making a large initial investment.

    Have you tried to make money on the internet? _____. If not what's stopping you? _____

2. The Internet should be used as a tool to create value and get paid. Use the internet as a tool, not as an end.

    Have you effectively used the internet as a tool to create opportunities for yourself and others? _____.

3. Dependent upon your business model, some internet opportunities might make you rich, others may barely breakeven.

    Write down your internet business model, strategy and how you plan to further your financial prosperity using the internet?

    _____
    _____
    _____
    _____

4. Most business models make money from the internet in one of three ways: advertising, subscriptions or straight sales.

    Which model works best for you? _____

5. One way to garner subscription revenue is to run a virtual marketplace. These sites make money by allowing buyers and sellers easy access to each other.

   List potential products or services you can advertise on the internet for subscription revenue? i.e. book-of-the-month club, recipe-of-the-month, etc.

   a. _____
   b. _____
   c. _____
   d. _____

6. The key master key to making money on the Internet is **connectivity.**

   What groups of people need to be connected to another group of people? i.e. business professionals with church groups, ABC Company with potential clients, etc.

   _____
   _____
   _____
   _____
   _____

7. The most exciting opportunity in this new millennium is *information marketing*. An entrepreneur whose main product is information is called an infopreneur.

8. Continually ask the question, "What else can I do for you."

   List three influential people you can ask.

   a. _____
   b. _____
   c. _____

Life Changing Answers Available in This Chapter

1. How can I get rid of fear, forever?

2. How can I use fear to help advance my vision financially?

3. Where does the fear of failure come from?

4. What are 10 other dangerous fears attached to the fear of failure?

Chapter 9

CONQUERING THE LAST ENEMY

Courage means controlling your fear.

At 2 a.m. in the morning, my three year old daughter yelled a loud terrifying scream in her bedroom, "Daddy, I just had a dream of a big green dinosaur with big blue spots! It had a pink bow and he was coming to eat me."

By the time I got to Gabrielle's room, she was shaking uncontrollably with paralyzing fear. Of course, it was nightmare. But to her, the nightmare was real.

Upon inquiry of her nightmare, I realized she dreamt about a harmless children television program called Barney. In case you don't have children, Barney is a purple dinosaur on PBS teaching children the value of relationship and education. He talks, sings and dances in ways children around the world love. My wife and I believed that Barney is a wonderful teaching tool for children, but Barney led the way to my daughter's nightmare. Come to find out, it was Barney's sidekick, "Baby Bop", that is green with big spots and a pink bow. Gabrielle watched the program earlier in the day and the images from the show transformed into her dream. That fear affected her sleep.

My daughter created something fearful, frightening and worrisome from something good. Until we got to the source of my daughter's nightmare, the negative fearful thoughts could have possibly haunted my daughter throughout her childhood.

Most of our fears haunt us consistently. And, the anxiety can come from a real place. Perhaps you watched someone lose their job or saw a beloved couple get a divorce. Maybe you worked for a company that went bankrupt or started a business that failed.

The "What if" syndrome plagues many hard working adults: "What if I lose my job?" "What if I get sick?" "What if I lose my house?" "What if..." These types of worrisome thoughts are always unproductive and can lead to a life full of the fear of failure.

No More Fear

Let's first define fear. A **fear** is an abnormal, persistent apprehension of situations, objects, activities, or persons. The main symptom of this disorder is the excessive, unreasonable desire to avoid the feared subject.

The operative word that hinders success in our definition above is "apprehension". Fear creates worry, hesitation, dread and anxiety. These unhealthy terms are direct enemies to your personal success and outward significance.

Throughout history all great human achievement has been accomplished by people who faced their fears, acted in the face of uncertainty and still dared to move forward. These people were no different from you or me. They had a particular fear, but learned to control it and overcome it, so that they could move their lives forward rather than allowing those fears to hold them back.

Why is fear of failure dangerous to your success?

1. The fear of failure will negatively control your life.

2. The fear of failure is a learned behavior that is debilitating to your future.

3. The fear of failure prevents your uniqueness from coming through.

1. The fear of failure could negatively control your life.

I have spent most of my life being controlled and motivated by the fear of failure. It has negatively affected virtually every area of my life. Where did it come from? And, what is the solution?

Since we are largely controlled by our dominant emotions, if you have experienced things in the past which created fear within you, then that fear will, to varying degrees, control your life and dictate your future actions. And if you have been raised as a child to be fearful, it will manifest itself in the form of some kind of restriction on your life as an adult.

The fear or method set up by you to control your fears prevents you from doing or achieving the things you would like to do, thereby preventing you from realizing your full potential.

Robert's solution. *If fear is a natural reaction to avoid something, then the opposite to fear is a natural desire to experience or accept something. Simply put, experiencing the* *thing you fear will lessen the power of the fear and in many cases destroy it.*

When your life is driven by love, it is expressed as desire, and strong desires will always overcome any fears you may have. For example, if your house is burning down a natural reaction would be to fear the fire because it could burn you. However if your son or daughter was inside the house, your love for them, and the desire created by that love, would more than likely be strong enough to overcome that fear and save your child.

Likewise with your personal success, your love for what you do for a living should help you overcome any obstacle that may lie in your way. When you truly love and believe in yourself, your desire will be strong enough to overcome any fear of failure. Your love for creating, helping, consulting or whatever you do should be the catalyst to experience the joy of it rather than avoiding or dreading it. This means that you are able to control yourself, rather than your fear controlling you.

> Courage means controlling your fear. Sometimes, you just need to do things "by faith."

Later on you will find out ways of dealing with these fears. However for now, you must learn to put yourself in a position to do what you love so that you can break free from the shackles of fear. That's why you are reading this book.

2.   The fear of failure is a learned behavior that is devastating to your future.

Did you know that you were born with two natural in-built fears? Every human was born with a fear of falling and a fear of loud noises. These fears were built into your DNA, and passed from generation to generation as a survival mechanism. Their only purpose was to keep you alive, by alerting you to potential dangers and creating an emotion within you that motivates you to avoid danger. You were not born with any other fears or phobias.

Now think about the implications of this, and the fears you currently have. If you were not born with the fears you have today, where did they come from? The answer is that at some point in your life you acquired them. Some event in your past caused you to associate a pain or danger with whatever it is you now fear, and now you are strongly motivated to avoid experiencing those emotions again.

When I was twelve years old, our house burned down to the ground. I remember the police picking me up from school and taking me to our smoldering home. There were four fire trucks pouring water on what now was rubble. And, there was my father on his knees crying in agony.

As a young adult, I didn't want to own a home out of my fear of one day losing it to a fire. I took on my family's burden of rebuilding our lives. What I didn't realize is eventually this experience turned into a fear of failure. I never wanted to own a house until I married my wife and she convinced me to overcome my fear of failure.

Robert's solution. *Because fear is learned, it can be can unlearned. Just as you learned to be fearful and apprehensive, you can learn to be successful and wealthy. But first you need to understand your fear, what caused your fear and what options are available to you to overcome it. We'll discuss the solutions in the next section of this chapter.*

145

3. *The Fear of failure prevents your uniqueness from coming through.*

I've spent most of my life trying to be like some other author or speaker or business guy. And, I've always failed. After many years of going from one failed project to the next, what I've learned is that a major part of my success is my uniqueness as a person.

Your uniqueness acts as your blueprint for what you are capable of achieving in life. And because you are different, no one can achieve exactly the same thing as you, in exactly the same way. What this means is that every person on earth has the potential to achieve something great, something only their uniqueness allows them to do. The fear of failure prevents your uniqueness from shinning through.

> Experiencing the thing that you fear will lessen its power over you and in many cases destroy it.

Most people are fearful of being themselves because they fear people will not like them. There is only one place where your fulfillment and contentment resides and you can only get to that place. Your unique personality, talents, gifts and skills can take you to that place.

Robert's solution. *Express your uniqueness in everything you do. Become satisfied and content with the way God made you and with who you are. By ignoring your own blueprint, you are essentially ignoring your own potential greatness. Later, we shall explore some ways of overcoming the fear that is holding you back from realizing your unique potential to stop chasing a paycheck.*

Getting To The Source

Fears come from three places.

- Outer Fear
- Inner Fear
- Subconscious Fear

Outer Financial Fear

Perhaps the most easily recognized fear is outer fear. This type of fear is caused by something you see with your physical senses. These fears are usually called phobias and can negatively affect your financial life.

Some examples of phobias, or extreme external fears, could include a fear of flying, a fear of rats, or a fear of big dogs. Generally speaking, all these fears tend to occur after some negative experience with them in the past.

For example, as a child I had a Labrador retriever as a pet. I took him for long walks and played with him in the back yard. However, as a teenager, I saw two pit bulls fighting and heard one of the dogs howling with pain. It was the most frightful sight I have ever witnessed and an even worst sound to hear.

As an adult, a wonderful family moved next door to our home in Atlanta. The neighbor came out to greet me and all of a sudden a golden retriever came from their backyard and ran to me with glee. His tail was waging with joy as he sniffed and licked my shoes. I was frozen with fear. The neighbor didn't speak with me for a year out of offense that I didn't like his dog.

Since that experience, plus a few other bad experiences with dogs, I have come to associate all dogs with the pain and discomfort I felt as a teenager. In other words, those bad experiences taught me that dogs were bad and I should avoid them. They taught me to fear dogs.

Financially speaking, if you have had a negative experience with money, it could affect your financial future. For example, if you had a car to be repossessed or a foreclosure or perhaps someone has stolen money from you, a phobia concerning money could hamper your relationship with money.

Fortunately, external fears are relatively simple in principle to overcome (though by no means easy!) providing you have a lot of determination and courage. Later in this chapter, we shall explore some techniques you can use to overcome these external fears.

Inner Financial Fear

Inner fear is something outside of you that you link a negative emotion to. This typically manifests itself as low self esteem, whereby you doubt your own worth to do or have something. Low self esteem is often a reflection of how someone treated you as a child, and the things you experienced throughout your life.

The most important and influential years, in terms of character development, are your early childhood and teenage years of life. You mind is most impressionable and still developing during your teenage years.

However, it is important to understand that most parents do not deliberately try to harm their child's self-esteem and make their children fearful later in life, but it happens often during the developmental years. For example, in an effort to discipline and guide a child through life, a parent may spank or send their child to the "naughty chair" to teach them a life lesson or as punishment.

Of course, discipline is certainly necessary in raising emotionally balanced children. An overbalanced amount of criticism and punishment can lead to feelings of rejection, fear of failure, inadequacy, lack of self-worth and self-doubt; other words, low self esteem.

A healthy balance of praise, love and affection is equally important to ensure fearful feelings are not carried throughout a child's life.

Some people associated with inner financial fear become hoarders of money and things with the fear of one day being punished with poverty.

Subconscious Financial Fear

Do you know someone who has sabotaged their own careers by doing something stupid? Self sabotage occurs when a person believes they are achieving more than they should. If they are close to success or even experience success for a short period of time, they always do something to "mess it up". It is likely there is something in their subconscious that is leading to them to a life of self-sabotage.

A subconscious fear is a belief that has been accepted by your subconscious mind, usually as a result of something you experienced or were told as a child. Perhaps a grade school teacher or coach said, "You always will be average." Or a misguided parent said, "You'll never do anything positive with your life." Or a jealous friend said, "You're stupid." Somehow these words may have gotten into your subconscious without your knowing about it.

As a result, these "subconscious fears" motivate you (*at the subconscious level*) to avoid this change or event, and go back to where you subconsciously believe you should be.

A good example of this can be found with money. A large majority of lottery winners spend all their money within a few years, and end up back where they started before they won the jackpot.

Because of their limiting subconscious beliefs that told them they were unworthy of such wealth, their subconscious takes them back to the level they subconsciously believed they should be by getting rid of all their millions.

> **Robert's solution.** *Check your "subconscious thermostat" by checking your self-talk. Are you constantly talking negative to yourself? Phrases like "I'm never going to get ahead." or "I'm a failure." Or "Nobody really likes me". This type of negative self-talk normally comes from your subconscious. Change your self-talk and you'll see a positive change in your attitude.*

Getting Rid of the Fear of Failure, Forever

As mentioned at the beginning of this chapter, it is important to understand the source of the Fear of Failure. This section will help you find, determine and solve forever your phobias. Let's first re-visit our definition of fear:

> *A **fear** is an abnormal, persistent apprehension of situations, objects, activities, or persons. The main symptom of this disorder is the excessive, unreasonable desire to avoid the feared subject.*

The term *phobia* is also used in a non-medical sense for aversions of all sorts and types of fears. A number of neologisms have appeared with the suffix -phobia, which are not phobias in the clinical sense, but rather describe a negative attitude towards something.

The list of fears below is associated with the fear of failure. The list may seem a light hearted look at phobias but for many people these are very real and damaging. The good news is that it doesn't have to be the way you think. If you locate symptoms in one of the areas, my suggestion is to get immediate counseling. You are the only one with the influence to change your perceptions. However, I want to walk you through a process that enables you to do so.

Fears Associated with the Fear of Failure

- Fear of people or the public
- Fear of being ridiculed
- Fear of new things or ideas
- Fear of money
- Fear of time
- Fear and avoidance of having to commit to anything, especially relationships
- Fear of public speaking
- Fear of responsibility
- Fear of possible defeat
- Fear of poverty

Tips and Solutions

The fear of people or the public is an extreme, pathological form of shyness. Shyness is a form of fear. It may be manifested in fears of looking people in the eye, avoiding one-on-one situations, shunning eating in public, afraid to develop relationships, and uneasiness when appearing in public.

Robert's Tip: If you are uncomfortable being around people, try to establish why you feel this way. Do you have a low opinion of yourself? Are you overly sensitive to criticism? Here are some tips: Make eye contact, don't belittle yourself, don't apologize for being the way you are, stand close to people to display confidence, use open-ended questions, and think about the good things you have to offer people.

The Fear of being ridiculed. Receiving criticism isn't always fun. However there are ways to handle it in a less hurtful way and – sometimes - get something good out of it.

Robert's Tip: Take praise and criticism evenly. If there is nothing to be learned from some piece of criticism you received or it's just jealous insults then shrug it off and put it out of your mind. Relative to print ridicule like email or newspapers, if you know it's coming, it's best that you don't read it or pay attention to it all.

Fear of new things or ideas. This type of fear produces an unwillingness to try new things or break away from routine. It is a reluctance to break free from pre-established thoughts.

Robert's Tip: Try something new every day. For example, take a different route to work tomorrow. Purchase a magazine outside of your normal interests. Send a thank you email to someone that's been kind to you. Attend a networking function that you would normally turn down.

The fear of money. They worry that they might mismanage money or that money might live up to its reputation as "the root of all evil." Some believe that money is actually evil so they despise it or fear it. Perhaps they remember well the ill fortune that befell the mythical King

Midas. His wish that everything he touched be turned to gold was fulfilled, and even his food was transformed into gold.

> ***Robert's Tip:*** Money by itself is not the root of all evil. The Bible says in 1 Timothy 6:10, "The love of money is the root of all evil." Loving money will lead to disappointment. You must understand that money is just a tool to help you advance your purpose. Learn all you can about managing money. Money should be your servant not your master.

The fear of time is an exaggerated or irrational fear of time. Prisoners often develop a fear of time passing.

> ***Robert's Tip:*** Spend all of your free time wisely. Become consumed with not wasting time. Turn the television off and read a book. Limit your internet surfing to a few moments a day and spend more time with family. Time will become your friend if you respect it and use it wisely.

The fear and avoidance of having to commit to anything, especially in relationships. These people can be torn between two worlds. They avoid obligations, ties, and commitments;   yet at the same time the commitment phobic may secretly crave the lives of those who are committed to others and the growth found in relationships.

> ***Robert's Tip:*** The foundation of this fear is the avoidance of making a bad decision or limiting one's options. In this case, the best policy would be to ensure that you are straightforward and honest with those involved with you. To play games and leave people waiting for your decision will only further frustration to your commitment issues.

The fear of speaking in public. The clinical term for the fear of public speaking is glossophia which comes from the Greek word, *glossa*, meaning tongue, and *phobos*, meaning fear or dread. To be a competent leader in any aspect, this fear must be overcome for people to follow you.

> *Robert's Tip:* The best way to conquer this fear is face it head on. Invite a few people over to your home or office. Depending upon the time of the meeting, serve them light snacks or drinks. Prepare and memorize a short speech perhaps on a topic that you speak from the heart, like "The Value of Friendships". Because they are friends, let them in on what you are doing. I would then recommend that you join Toastmasters or Dale Carnegie which specializes in helping participant overcome stage freight. The secret key to overcoming this fear, however, is preparation.

The fear of responsibility. As our culture increasingly glorifies the carefree pleasures of youth, many people grow despondent when the reality of adult responsibility pulls them farther away from their youthful hopes and expectations.

> *Robert's Tip:* It comes down to redirecting your unconscious mind from being a youngster to developing into an adult. To be an adult means taking responsibility for yourself, your family and community. On the surface, you know your hypegiaphobia is illogical. But it has persisted because your subconscious has attached the idea of responsibility to all those negative emotions. Perhaps in your spare time, you can volunteer at the local shelter or a department at your church.

The fear of failure or defeat. As life becomes more complicated and peer pressure grows strong, this can push you into a world where competition is very high. It plagues your mind, thus deterring you from thinking logically. The fear may erupt for many reasons; like fear of marriage, fear of being a bad parent, fear of failing to get a good job, or fear of not getting promoted all of which can cloud the mind and stop you from reaching any concrete decision.

Fear of failure, or the clinical term Kakorrhaphiophobia, tends to overpower your life. Frustration, anger, disappointment, discouragement, self-sabotages and stress are always associated with this disorder. It will ruin key relationships and financial success.

> *Robert's Tip:* If you are a competitive person, set reasonable goals for yourself, not against what others are doing. Stand in the mirror and stay there until you get comfortable with everything you see; then walk away content with who you are and the way God made you (including the flaws you see). From there, work on yourself a little at a time. Be free to talk with those around you and embrace life as it comes. Remember; do not compare yourself (financially or professionally) to anyone. It's never worth the headache.

The fear of poverty, clinically known as peniaphobia, is an exaggerated or irrational fear of losing everything.

> *Robert's Tips:* - I watched on the news not long ago about a billionaire who sleeps with the light on in his bedroom out of fear that he might wake up and all of his possessions will be gone. This type of fear is tormenting. To help conquer this fear, become a giver to charities, foundations, churches and outreach programs. The more you give, the more comfortable you will be with having possessions. If you are stingy or a hoarder, your fear of losing it all will only increase as you continue in this manner. It's great to have possessions as long as possessions don't control your thoughts.

Are you ready to put these solutions, answers and antidotes to use? Courage means controlling your fear and advancing your vision with all of your might.

Chapter Principles
And My Personal Challenges to You

1. Throughout history all great human achievement has been accomplished by people who faced their fears, acted in the face of uncertainty and still dared to move forward.

    Has fear kept you from achieving what you know is possible in your life? _____

2. A **fear** is an abnormal, persistent apprehension of situations, objects, activities, or persons.

    How would you define fear?
    _____
    _____

3. If fear is a natural reaction to avoid something, then the opposite to fear is a natural desire to experience or accept something.

    Knowing that God loves you, how do you intend to use your faith in God to overcome the stress of fear the next time it may arise?
    _____
    _____
    _____
    _____

4. Most people are fearful of being themselves because they fear people will not like them.

    Are you comfortable or fearful with who you are, what you look like and what you have become? _____

5. A subconscious fear is a belief that has been accepted by your subconscious mind, usually as a result of something you experienced or were told as a child.

    Write down the words that God says about you? i.e. "prosperous", "His favorite child", "wonderfully-made", etc.

    - _____
    - _____
    - _____
    - _____
    - _____
    - _____
    - _____
    - _____
    - _____

6. Fear doesn't have to control your life.

    What are three things you can do today to face your greatest fears?

    a. _____
    b. _____
    c. _____

    Do it today.

7. You are the only one with the influence to change your perceptions.

8. When your life is driven by love, it is expressed as desire, and strong desires will always overcome any fears you may have.

LIVE LIFE ON YOUR OWN TERMS

I pray that you may prosper in every way,
even as your soul (mind) prospers. ~ 3 John 2

A lot of people talk about financial success, wealth-building and economic prosperity.

You hear it often on cable news. Analysis will say, "Now is the time to buy stocks while the prices are low." On Sunday morning, your preacher may shout, "God wants you to prosper". Or a friend say, "Buy my products and you'll be rich."

Total life prosperity includes money but is not limited to money. Prosperity includes good health, a loving family and obedient children. The very definition of prosperity is the ability to have options. The more prosperity you have the more options will be at your command such as taking a paid in full vacation, or hiring a new employee and giving a thousand dollars to your church. Total life prosperity begins when you transition into your life's purpose, express it in everything you do and use it to help people get what they want. As you help others achieve you'll ultimately get the things you want.

Prosperity develops when you implement all the laws and principles of *Never Chase A Paycheck Again*. It will allow you to live life on your terms, not someone else's. The more principles you put in practice, the sooner your opportunities to prosper will develop.

I hope you have enjoyed learning about these powerful principles to finance your life. More important, I hope they will help you develop the prosperous life of your dreams. Embrace them and share them with others, especially young adults. Your life will never be the same again. That's my promise to you!

NOTES

Kings & Priests Unlimited

A Lifelong Partner Dedicated to
Lifting Your Potential

Kings & Priests Unlimited, a 501(c)3 non-profit organization, dedicates itself to empowering and educating individuals and organizations across America and around the world. It accomplishes this mission by forging lasting partnerships to foster personal growth and organization effectiveness.

Kings & Priests consists of:

- **ReignMakers Mentor Program for Adults** – Using the latest technology, Robert Watkins personally mentors and coaches individuals to extraordinary levels of success and prosperity.
- **Conquer Worldwide Conferences** – Empowers corporate and church leaders to marketplace success.
- **Conquer Consulting** – Business planning services for aspiring entrepreneurs and established businesses.
- **Young CEO Entrepreneurial Summer Camps** – Equips teenagers in character, business and finance.
- **Robert Watkins Ministries** – Teaching, training and ministering for church congregations and conferences.

To contact Robert Watkins:

3600 Dallas Hwy, Ste 230
PMB 227
Marietta, GA 30064
www.ConquerWorldwide.com (web)
info@conquerworldwide.com (email)

About the Author

Robert Watkins
Business Strategist · Growth Consultant · Speaker

A popular conference speaker in great demand relative to marketplace, finance and personal success topics, Robert is known for his innovative presentations, solid content, and practical application, spiced with the right amount of humor. Robert leaves his congregations and audiences ready to take action! He launched Robert Watkins Ministries to teach churches and corporations how to experience financial and entrepreneurial freedom.

Robert served in the **United States Army** and graduated from **West Georgia University.** He also founded Conquer Worldwide, which has mentored and educated thousands of aspiring entrepreneurs, professionals and business owners. After retiring from Corporate America in his 30's, he launched the non-profit organization, **Kings & Priests Unlimited in 2001**, which has trained thousands of Christian leaders for financial freedom, leadership development and business success. He then founded **Young Leaders Unlimited**, a character-development program for teenagers.

Robert also received an honorary **doctorate degree** in business and theology and has spoken at many higher learning institutions including Harvard School of Business, Emory Business School and West Georgia University to name a few. He has written several best-selling books and programs including *Be Your Own Boss, How To Hear From God,* and *Never Chase a Paycheck Again.*

With all of Robert's successes, his greatest joy is his family. **Married for 18 years** to Evelyn Watkins; they are raising two beautiful daughters in the Atlanta area.

For more information about Robert Watkins' broad range of services, including the Reign Makers Mentors Program, speaking engagements, business and church consulting, training and published materials (videos, CDs, manuals, training outlines), please contact:

Robert Watkins
3600 Dallas Hwy, Ste 230
PMB 227
Marietta, GA 30064

1.888.378.5554 (tel)
1.404.601.9692 (fax)

www.ConquerWorldwide.com (website)
info@ConquerWorldwide.com (email)